MW00817948

THE SACRIFICED LIFE:
Keys to Intimacy with God

God bless you!

Bobby

(Ruth 2:12)

THE
SACRIFICED
LIFE

Keys to
Intimacy
with God

Bobby Welch

BROADMAN PRESS
NASHVILLE, TENNESSEE

© Copyright 1992 • Broadman Press
All rights reserved

4210-18
ISBN: 0-8054-1018-X

Dewey Decimal Classification: SPIRITUAL LIFE
Subject Heading: 248

Library of Congress Catalog Card Number: 92-5010

Printed in the United States of America

Unless otherwise stated, all Scripture quotations are from the *King James Version of the Bible*.

Scripture quotations marked NASB are from *The New American Standard Bible*. © The Lockman Foundation, 1960, 1962, 1963, 1968, 1971, 1972, 1973, 1975, 1977. Used by permission.

Scripture quotations marked TLB are taken from *The Living Bible*. Copyright © Tyndale House Publishers, Wheaton, Illinois, 1971. Used by permission.

Scripture quotations marked NIV are from the Holy Bible, *New International Version*, copyright © 1973, 1978, 1984 by International Bible Society.

Scripture quotations marked GNB are from the *Good News Bible*, the Bible in Today's English Version. Old Testament: Copyright © American Bible Society 1976; New Testament: Copyright © American Bible Society 1966, 1971, 1976. Used by permission.

Library of Congress Cataloging-in-Publication Data

Welch, Bobby, 1943-
    The sacrificed life : keys to intimacy with God / Bobby Welch.
      p.   cm.
    ISBN 0-8054-1018-X
    1. Christian life—1960-   I. Title.
BV4501.2.W4166   1992
248.4—dc20   92-5010
                                       CIP

DEDICATION

To all those believers who have remained unnamed and unnoticed upon this earth because they truly learned and followed the way of THE SACRIFICED LIFE and thus became greatest in the Kingdom of heaven, especially those who make up the suffering church of martyrdom . . .

To that part of Christ's Body that is mostly unseen and unheard, forgotten, suffering, persecuted, underground, and often martyred—our own brothers and sisters from whom I have most clearly seen that *The Sacrificed Life* is *the only way* to follow Christ truly.

—Bobby Welch

THANK YOU, THANK YOU!

To THE FIRST BAPTIST CHURCH, DAYTONA BEACH, from whom I drew the encouragement and security to explore the Servant/Intercessor life, and from whom rose so many hidden heroes . . .

To MAUDELLEN, HAYLEE, AND MATTHEW, a family who has always so willingly shared the joys and some frustrations of a husband, father, and pastor searching for what many see as "the foolish way."

To MRS. PEGGY HARPER, a wonderful staff colaborer. Without her tireless efforts, attention to details, and continuous belief in the message of these pages, this book would likely never have become a reality.

CONTENTS

PART I

The Sacrificed Life Is a

DISCOVERY

Again, the kingdom of heaven is like unto a merchant man, seeking goodly pearls: Who, when he had found one pearl of great price, went and sold all that he had, and bought it.   *Matthew 13:45-46*

1 | A PERSONAL NOTE

The ministries of four men influenced my life at almost the same time; each man was from a different country (and seemingly almost different worlds). These diverse accents spoke from varying perspectives—all flowing into the reservoir from which the Lord was teaching me about what I have come to call "The Sacrificed Life." Later the Holy Spirit sent confirming lives and voices. These became the most searching and intense days filled with God's thrilling, but often embarrassing, searching of me.

Nothing can take the place of the Lighthouse that towers in the heavenlies, but the lower lights along the shore at water's edge are also wonderfully helpful to the searching sailor.

So it is with the sacrificed life. Nothing can substitute for the Word of God, the grace of God, and the Spirit of God in leading in the sacrificed life. But much appreciation is to those believers who have kept their spiritual "lower lights" bright along the shore where we live. They have, by His grace, afforded much guidance and confidence to this searcher.

These pages have come from my personal search. Despite working from rough personal notes, some from years past, I have tried to credit all possible contributors. However, some of the brightest "lower lights" have gone unnamed, unfamed, unprinted, unrecorded, and unpictured because of their own personal desire and deep understanding of the sacrificed life. Their rewards are on another shore where lowest lights are brightest. May, by His grace, others be brought to join that very illumination throughout all eternity because while upon this earth they, too, found and followed the sacrificed life.

These pages have been written for three basic reasons:

1. God poured out on me so much so fast that it seemed to go in my mind and out my mouth—but my hunger was for it to melt into my soul and life.

2. These lessons were helpful to others, and I needed to re-study for spiritual refreshment.

3. The elements of the sacrificed life need constantly to be reviewed.

If there is any "uniqueness" about these pages it would likely be that many truths we've known or suspected are systematically linked together in this volume to expose God's saving plan that is to be demonstrated in the life of each believer. Therefore, "The Sacrificed Life" is the one and only wise way for the believer who hungers and thirsts after righteousness.

"This is the way; follow therein!"

2 | A DWELLING PLACE

It seems as if I had emerged from a spiritual fog and come upon a place. This dwelling place was plain, but not drab—certainly not a palace or the like. Across it was the name and house number:

"Servants' Quarters"
(Matt. 20:25)

The windows are foggy or dusty, and I clear a spot to peer inside at a section of the servants' dwellings. What is inside is remarkable and amazing! Instead of seeing dead, dull slaves, it is exactly the opposite! From window to window I move discovering through each peephole another incredible aspect of life in the "Servants' Quarters." As I discover the joy of a life meant to be lived by the Master's servants as they deny self, sacrifice, and even suffer, my heart and lips quietly respond: "Wonderful, praise the Lord, and to think all along I and so many others have been drawing back from and dreading the unsure outcome of a devoted servant life, while all the while it is inside these very servants' quarters that the joy of the Lord seems to flow deepest."

What believer would not want to live among such colaborers and enjoy such a comaraderie of giving and sharing in the Master's name? This is the earthly dwelling place meant for all the redeemed.

But why aren't there more "followers of Christ" dwelling in the servants' quarters? It cannot be that such a servant's life is unattractive and uninviting because this was the very life our Master lived while here. This is the very dwelling place of Jesus upon earth. We may sleep in His bed, eat at His table, walk His way.

For me, it is not the fog. I have discovered the "Servants' Quarters" and see clearly enough to understand, that for my life here, this is where I should dwell. Yet I have not completely moved in! Perhaps I've ventured to crack the door or even stepped inside far enough to develop a series of lessons, but I do not yet dwell here as so many and as I yearn to do! But yet here it stands and our Lord and Master bids us come.

The following pages are the result of seeing more clearly, hearing my Master's call, and a deep longing to dwell consistently inside the servants' quarters. There is room for others, but to most it will appear to be the sacrificed life.

3 | THE "SACRIFICED LIFE" DEFINED

"A peculiar people" (Titus 2:14)

The message of the cross leads inescapably to a servant life which is exactly the opposite of the life-style of the world; therefore, the world calls the cross way sacrificial—hence The Sacrificed Life. Let the believer who walks that path be of good cheer when declared in The Sacrificed Life, for so they labeled Jesus:

> And many of them said, He hath a devil, and is mad; why hear ye him? (John 10:20).

> And when his friends heard of it, they went out to lay hold on him: for they said, He is beside himself (Mark 3:21).

Her fellow Christians labeled Rhoda as crazy.

> And they said unto her, Thou art mad (Acts 12:15).

And they labeled Paul and others:

> Paul, thou art beside thyself; much learning doth make thee mad. But he said, I am not mad, . . . but speak forth the words of truth and soberness (Acts 26:24-25).

> For whether we be beside ourselves, it is to God: or whether we be sober, it is for your cause (2 Cor. 5:13).

> I am become a fool in glorying (2 Cor. 12:11).

The Sacrificed Life is more than a onetime decision. It is an expedition that is filled with glorious joy and untold treasures. Such a peculiar people upon The Sacrificed Life begin and continue in a discovery, a desire, a discipline.

4 | AGES AND STAGES OF MATURITY

Beloved, I wish above all things that thou mayest prosper and be in health, even as thy soul prospereth (3 John 2).

The Christian life is one of joy, faith, obedience, doctrine, and even conflict. The Christian life is also one of growth in the Lord Jesus.

But we beseech you, brethren, that ye increase more and more (1 Thess. 4:10).

. . . may grow up into him in all things, which is the head, even Christ (Eph. 4:15).

Let us go on unto perfection; not laying again the foundation of repentance from dead works, and of faith toward God (Heb. 6:1).

As ye have therefore received Christ Jesus the Lord, so walk ye in him: Rooted and built up in him, and stablished in the faith, as ye have been taught, abounding therein with thanksgiving (Col. 2:6-7).

Church membership in America seems to be growing, but members largely are not. One reason for this, I believe, could be overdependence on others. Many believers who lack spiritual maturity blame the church's lack of programs, attention, and emphasis. While I'm sure this is true in some cases, the believer must be honest. Individual spiritual growth is an individual responsibility—with or without outside helps!

The Ethiopian eunuch and many others were not blessed with

15

elaborate systems of support, other than the Holy Spirit, to ensure their growth. Growth must be understood as a solo flight after learning to fly. Christians must be willing to pay the price for growth.

By spiritual growth, I do not mean growing in our standing before God. Justification is not a process. It happens the moment we receive, by grace alone, Jesus Christ as our Savior. We then grow and become more and more like Him.

Spiritual growth should be steady and consistent rather than a series of crisis experiences. We often find ourselves growing during a crisis, but crises are not to be our primary means of growth. If we make this mistake we are sure to end up chasing "spiritual rabbits."

Then too, we must be on guard to watch for what I will call "spiritual slippage." It's easy to move through the early stages of spiritual growth and have continual relapses, too many and too often.

In Hosea, God calls Israel a backslidden heifer. This is a picture of a cow standing but not budging to go forward. Spiritual growth is like riding a bicycle. We either go forward or we stop and stumble. One fellow commented, "I knew I was backslidden when I was unwilling to go forward." So true. If we're satisfied where we are spiritually, we're backslidden!

Positive Motivations for Growth

1. It is the will of God that we grow.
2. In order to be obedient we must grow.
3. We are predestined to be conformed to the image of Christ.
4. The Holy Spirit yearns for us to be like Christ. The Spirit will gnaw at us if we stagnate.
5. We're saved to victory and not to defeat. Satan should not be defeating us daily.
6. Rewards in heaven have a relationship to spiritual growth here.

Negative Motivations for Growth

1. When Satan hinders us, deadness sets in.
2. To keep from losing rewards in heaven.
3. To keep from living a negative life.
4. To avoid chastisement.

The Bible depicts basically four spiritual growth stages through which every normal, healthy believer should progress. These stages have almost no relationship to the biological age of the believer or length of time one has been converted. One may have been saved for thirty years and still be a spiritual babe. In other words, spiritual growth is based upon stages, not ages.

I heard Bobby Moore preach a message taken from Ezekiel 47:1-12, concerning the pilgrimage of the believer. He spoke of the believer's life as being in water. First one is ankle deep, knee deep, waist deep, and then over one's head, thus forcing him to swim.

These water levels parallel these four stages of spiritual growth as we spiritually advance. The following is a brief idea of these four stages.

Stage I:
Spiritual Babes

Most married couples want children. Imagine a couple who planned on having children. Later, however, the wife changed her mind and was no longer willing to have a baby. This would grieve the husband who had yearned to have children. So it is with Jesus, the Bridegroom, who becomes grieved and disappointed with us when we are unwilling to bear spiritual children. Babies are beautiful!

Characteristics of Healthy Spiritual Babies

1. They have been Christians a short time (usually less than a year and a half). They will have a desire to grow (1 Pet. 2:2).

2. They have walked down the aisle of a church, followed the Lord in believer's baptism, and perhaps become tithers.
3. They will have their own personal Bible, if Bibles are available.
4. They will be involved in Bible study, usually having more and more assurance of salvation, and likely obeying what they know is godly, regardless of what others are doing.
5. They will be interested in being around other believers.
6. They will be telling others about Jesus.

But babies are not so marvelous if they remain babies. In our church there is a wonderful couple whose only child had a disease that caused him never to grow. He lived like an infant in diapers for twenty-one years, and then he died. They called him "Little Son." That was such a tragedy, and it is a tragic picture of too many babes in Christ who never grow. The infant stage of spiritual growth is normal only for the newly saved.

A little girl who was soaked in a rainstorm came inside but stayed near the door rather than moving to the warmth of the fireplace. She became deathly sick because she was satisfied just being inside the door to escape the weather. She failed to come near the warmth she needed to be healthy and well. Just as the girl became sick, we, too, become spiritually sick when we stay barely inside the door of salvation.

> And I, brethren, could not speak unto you as unto spiritual, but as unto carnal, even as unto babes in Christ. I have fed you with milk, and not with meat: for hitherto ye were not able to bear it, neither yet now are ye able. For ye are yet carnal: for whereas there is among you envying, and strife, and divisions, are ye not carnal, and walk as men? (1 Cor. 3:1-3)

Christendom today is suffering because of, as R. G. Lee put it, Bantam Baptists, Minute Methodists, and Pygmy Presbyterians and Pentecostals. One reason the church is not doing better at winning the lost is because it has to spend so much time and resources changing diapers and feeding spiritual babies.

Sadly, many today should be driving chariots of fire but instead are being pushed in baby buggies! Many should be living cannonball experiences with God but have settled for popgun existences.

Stage II:
Spiritual Children

> I write unto you, little children, because your sins are forgiven you for his name's sake. . . . I write unto you, little children, because ye have known the Father (1 John 2:12-13).

Four Essentials in Childhood Growth

1. Food—the Word of God.
2. Air/breathing—the Word of God is what you breathe in and prayer is what you breathe out.
3. Exercise—*do* something. Don't just try to look good. Looks deceive.
4. Right atmosphere—place of warmth, truth, understanding, caring, concern, and love, which is the local church. A man who had been preaching for thirty years got into a "hornet's nest church," suffered many difficulties, and then got out. His next church was loving and kind and he was overcome with the contrast. We all need a place in which to grow.

> That we henceforth be no more children, tossed to and fro, and carried about with every wind of doctrine, by the sleight of men, and cunning craftiness, whereby they lie in wait to deceive. But speaking the truth in love, may grow up into him in all things, which is the head, even Christ (Eph. 4:14-15).

Stage III
Young Men (Adolescents)

> I write unto you, young men, because ye have overcome the wicked one. . . . I have written unto you, young men, because ye are strong, and the word of God abideth in you, and ye have overcome the wicked one (1 John 2:13-14).

There is a footnote in *The Open Bible* (NASB, p. 1169) concerning young men which reads, "Spiritual growth to that of a young man is not reached by many. He is strong and virile, and is well able to overcome his enemy. He has a vision for the future and the faith and courage to tackle it. He is preparing for his productive years. You, too, can become a young man spiritually by 'putting away childish things' and grow."

Strength is the most obvious characteristic of a young man. Older people are comical when trying to regain their youth. They may try, but they can never recapture the strength and vivacity of youth.

Jesus waxed strong in the spirit; Abraham grew strong in faith; we are to be strong in the Lord and in the power of His might.

The key to growing in strength and overcoming Satan is in verse 14. "The word of God lives in you" (NIV). So grasp that truth, and let it grasp you! Let the Word come alive in your life.

"Beloved, I wish that above all things that thou mayest prosper and be in health, even as thy soul prospereth" (3 John 2). Many, however, would be in bad shape if God answered that prayer. What a compliment to Gaius, what a curse to many of the people called Christians! I'm afraid if our physical health really corresponded to the condition of our souls, we would not be prospering.

There is a condition which I call the "spiritual mid-life crisis." It occurs between childhood and adolescence. One goes to sleep there, becoming stagnant. The devil accomplishes this by getting us to compare ourselves with others. He reveals the lost world and even lost members in the church and says, "See, you're not so bad." Of course we agree, because, after all, we're no longer spiritual babes, we're growing! Then he reveals the carnal Christians. (Sadly, too many times, Satan can point to a carnal pastor, staff member, or leader for our comparison.) We say, "Why, *I'm* doing great!" Satan will also encourage you to compare your early spiritual adolescence to that of some spiritual "fathers" who are perceived as "foolish" by the world and by many Christians. No one wants to be called a "fool!" After comparing ourselves to the lost world, lost church members, carnal Christians, and some "foolish" believers, we appear to be doing great, and we sit down at the early stages of spiritual adolescence and never grow. It has been my observation that spiritual adolescence is the point at which the vast majority of Christendom remains today.

To counter Satan's deceit, we should compare ourselves to the Word of God and the life of Christ. By doing this, we will begin to proceed in our spiritual growth.

Average Christianity today is not "normal" Christianity. It is not what God intended. It is not that for which Christ died. It is tragic to see an inactive church in the midst of a lost and dying world that so desperately needs to see and hear Christ.

Stage IV:
Spiritual Fathers

I write to you, fathers, because you have known him who is from the beginning (1 John 2:14, NIV).

At this fourth and final stage, the believer is coming into spiritual maturity—fatherhood. The spiritually mature person is not sanctimonious and superficial. This is not the "spotlight," usually enjoyed by babes and toddlers. The spiritual father abides in the law, Spirit, and Word of God. He has set out to allow Christ to live through him. My experience has been that he must be sought out because he seeks no recognition. Further, I'm convinced that he dies in worldly obscurity because of his commitment to decrease that Jesus may increase. In fact, it may be that the most mature believer considers himself the least spiritual because of his intimacy to the holiness of God.

Spiritual maturity is a growth process and not an instantaneous happening. To grow a tomato, one puts a seed into the ground, cultivates it, and nurtures it. First, there appears a blossom and we become excited. We marvel over it for awhile. The flowers indicate there is something going on inside, and there is more to come! We continue to cultivate and nurture the plant. Then one day after this painstaking process—a tomato appears! If we don't understand this process and the excitement over the blossoms, we will lose sight that there is more to come—the fruit. Remember, some pruning is always required.

Most believers do not understand and cannot accept, with joy, God's pruning process because they do not fully grasp the growth process.

What is our goal? How will we know when we're seeing fruit and not just flowers? First consider these verses:

> Till we all come in the unity of the faith, and of the knowledge of the Son of God, unto a perfect man, unto the measure of the stature of the fullness of Christ: That we henceforth be no more children, tossed to and fro, and carried about with every wind of doctrine, by the sleight of men, and cunning craftiness, whereby they lie in wait to deceive (Eph. 4:13-14).

> Be kindly affectioned one to another with brotherly love; in honor preferring one another (Rom. 12:10).

Consequently we will begin to take on more of a family likeness. We will look more and more like the Father and Jesus to whom we belong.

The fifteenth chapter of John contains the teaching of the vine and branches. In it we read, "I in you [and you in me]. . . . without me ye can do nothing" (vv. 4-5). It is essential to understand our position. Our sap-sharing and fruit-bearing depend on our abiding in Him.

At salvation we are in Him. Paul says, "That I may . . . be found in him" (Phil. 3:9, NIV). But beyond that are verses like the following: "He that saith he abideth in him ought himself also to walk, even as he walked" (1 John 2:6). "These things have I written unto you that believe on the name of the Son of God; that ye may know that ye have eternal life, and that ye may believe on the name of the Son of God" (5:13).

There is a reciprocal relationship indicated here. We can picture such a relationship when we say that the poker is in the fire and the fire is in the poker; or the sponge is in the water and the water is in the sponge; and we're in the air and the air is in us.

Paul wanted to be in Him like the poker is in the fire and the fire is in the poker. Wherever Christ is found, we should be there; wherever we are found, Christ should be there. If we are maturing, we will be found in Jesus—in the traffic jam, on Saturday night, dealing with pesky people, or during disasters, setbacks, and reversals. In the very best and the very worst, the world finds Jesus walking and speaking in and through us.

Too many people in the church today want to be amused by the "dog and pony shows." In contrast, people in the early church were not amused but amazed at what Jesus was doing in them.

The world today has plenty of amusement. But what people really need is to be amazed by Jesus through spiritually mature believers. These believers will win people to Christ and send them on their own growing, glowing way in the Lord! "For other foundation can no man lay than that is laid, which is Jesus Christ" (1 Cor. 3:11).

Some Characteristics of "Father" Christians

Have a definite personal ministry which the Lord is blessing.

Have a daily and quality time spent in prayer and Bible reading.

Pray to become humble.

Understand and welcome brokenness.

Have a greater capacity for patience and endurance.

Daily deny yourself for Jesus.

Lose your life for Christ's sake.

Share in or have fellowship in the sufferings of Jesus.

Sincerely rejoice at the very time you are going through personal hardship and trials and have confidence that God will work good.

Allow your sufferings to shape, strengthen, and even lead to the salvation of those around you.

Characterize the normal way of your life by Galatians 5:22-26.

Fill your mind with things that are true, just, pure, lovely, and of good report (Phil. 4:8).

As a rule, go directly to those who may have something
   against you and try to be reconciled.
Examine the fruits of your labor.

In my study, I have been able to find volumes of material about
the first two stages of growth and some on the third, but virtually
nothing on the fourth stage. Few, it seems, have reached that
stage of spiritual development, and those that have continue to
go unrecognized because they have decreased as He has increased.

"But what things were gain to me, those I counted loss for
Christ" (Phil. 3:7).

What is our great spiritual yearning? "That I may win
Christ, . . . be found in him, . . . and know him." Paul is talking
about our potential as well as our position in Him (vv. 8-10).

The process of spiritual maturity involves a spiritual warfare
and continual battle. A baby doesn't want a battle, he wants a
bottle. A baby doesn't want a sword, he wants a sucker. A baby
doesn't want a duty, he wants a diaper change. We must begin to
take up the sword in this life, respond to the call of duty, move
out, and do battle victoriously in Jesus. After all, we should and
can be even "more than conquerors"! (Rom. 8:37).

Such a victorious life travels along the two parallel tracks of
desire and *discipline* which we will soon consider. Those tracks
ensure a continual supply to the "new man" within us.

5 | Essential Elements of Intimacy

As a scout platoon leader in Vietnam my main responsibility was to track the enemy, observe him at close range, and report information back to headquarters. There was much to see, learn, observe, and report. However, there was a basic requirement that was always sought back at the commander's headquarters. This basic information was termed as E.E.I.—Essential Elements of Information.

For the believer to be in right relationship with his Commander, he, too, needs to understand at least the basic E.E.I.— Essential Elements of *Intimacy, yes, Intimacy.* The Lord has no favorites, but He does have intimates. And there are some absolute requirements for our close intimate companionship and victory in the Lord Jesus! The *three essential elements of intimacy* can be brought down to three simple words: *Alone, obey,* and *word.*

The First Essential Element of Intimacy: Aloneness

It was the habit of Jesus to be alone with the Father. "And when he had sent the multitudes away, he went up into a mountain apart to pray: and when the evening was come, he was there alone" (Matt. 14:23).

The Lord wants you and me. He is not merely interested in our church attendance, money, and membership any more than a woman in love would only want her husband's name, pay-

25

check, and house. She wants her husband and time alone with him, often.

The Lord wants you, and He wants time alone with you, often! He has wonderful, intimate secrets and affections to share— but only alone. The only person who would argue with such truth is the one who has not often spent time alone with Him.

We are not talking about scraps, bits, or tiny pieces of time but much time. Hours per day! Do not struggle against such a suggestion. Everyone will give a reasonable excuse to avoid such discipline, all except those who have experienced that intimacy. Books and pamphlets abound which tell us how to spend thirty minutes, five minutes, three minutes, and even one minute alone with God. Of course, any moment with the Lord is precious, but we must have more time alone with Him. The reason we need much time with Him is not that we are so deep to be filled but rather we have so many cracks, holes, and leaks!

Dear God, give us a way to spend hours daily with You alone!

A Principle

This aloneness with God is a biblical principle with which we are confronted. "But Martha was cumbered about much serving, and came to him, and said, Lord, dost thou not care that my sister hath left me to serve alone? Bid her therefore that she help me. And Jesus answered and said unto her, Martha, Martha, thou art careful and troubled about many things: But one thing is needful: and Mary hath chosen that good part, which shall not be taken away from her" (Luke 10:40-42). "And this I speak for your own profit; not that I may cast a snare upon you, but for that which is comely, and that ye may attend upon the Lord without distraction" (1 Cor. 7:35).

The frank truth of life is that many believers will not be around this time next year (if they do not soon learn and practice this principle). And many believers who do remain will continue entangled in the numbness of dead, dry spiritual motions instead of a soul afire as the two on the Emmaus road. Someone has said, "Come apart or come apart." That is true. Ah, alone, that is where we shall devote ourselves to what David Brainard, a saint of sacred solitude, called "those sacred duties!"

A People

A host of people provide the indisputable evidence that God pours out Himself to those who love Him and spend time alone with Him.

Abraham as continually being called away to follow and be God's—alone. He was called from Ur of the Chaldees, called from Haran, and called from Lot. God seemed to be saying, "Come closer, closer, closer to Me, I have some secrets to share." And when God spoke He did not send the message first to Lot in Sodom but to Abraham, alone with God.

Moses is remembered standing in victory at the Red Sea miracle. But before that there was the aloneness with the Lord in the Midian desert where he was reduced to humility and then upon holy ground where he heard God speak from a burning bush. Moses is remembered as standing in power with the tables of the law at Mount Sinai. Where did Moses receive that law? Down on his face, alone with God!

Elijah is remembered as being used of God to perform the first resurrection and later brought down fire from heaven upon the altar at Mount Carmel. But look back yonder "by the brook Cherith that is before Jordan" (1 Kings 17:3). There is Elijah, who had hidden himself alone with God!

David is remembered as the giant killer standing atop Goliath (1 Sam. 17). How did he come to such a victorious courage, faith, determination? Read verses 34-37, and you will see that such was not sudden, but rather a process that began with a lion and then a bear. Where did that happen? A shepherd lad by himself alone with the Lord (v. 37). Many believers, going with no hope whatsoever against giants, are being defeated on every side by spiritual toads, flesh, and grasshoppers. Much spiritual defeat is due to not getting alone with the Lord!

Paul, the apostle, is remembered for his courage, perseverance, and love for the lost. But we must not forget "many days"

when he "went into Arabia" (Gal. 1:17). Many believed this was
a time to be alone with the Lord which is thought to have occurred in Acts 9, between verses 22 and 23. Also there is no
doubt that Paul spent much time otherwise alone with the Lord.

Jesus is seen overcoming death with grace in front of a back-
drop of aloneness with the Father in the garden of Gethsemane.
All these and many others, then and throughout the ages, have
been singularly touched—alone with God.

Make no mistake. To be alone with God is a discipline that
exacts a price.

A Price

Everything within us will rise up and declare, "To be alone and
spend time with the Lord is not easy!" And nearly all mankind,
both lost and saved, will quickly assemble to add voices and volume to such a declaration. But no matter if all the earth should
agree, to be alone with the Lord is no less vital and the Holy Spirit
within one gives God's amen! Absolutely, it is not easy. It is a
matter of discipline. It is a matter of spiritual victory both coming
and going from our meeting time with our Majesty!

There is not a successful sportsman, musician, or businessman
that does not understand that every goal requires discipline, and
all discipline has a price tag. Even as I write these very lines I have
had to pay a price for the privilege to be alone to write and plead
for His breath upon these pages. But, as we are alone with Him
we know it is worth it all!

The following are a few necessities you will find listed on the
price invoice for private involvement with the Lord.

Doubtless, you must give up something. Your life and schedule are already packed. Some things must go. There are several
lessons from Jesus' teaching about plucking out and cutting off.
One fact (Matt. 5:29-30) is certain: Our Lord is saying it is far
better to be physically maimed than spiritually malnourished.
That which we must offer to be cut off is not a part of our body
but encumbrances that rob our bodies and spirits from time alone
with Him. Beware at this point. If you are not carefully led of

Christ you will throw out the very thing you need and keep the very thing that you do not need. Jeremiah 17:9 says, "The heart is, . . . desperately wicked: who can know it?" In all likelihood He will not remove you from your family or from the place in which you work in His vineyard. No, He often leads us to cut closer to our own bones in the area of our own selfish and self-serving delights. Ask the Lord to show you what must go. He will. He's been waiting for you to ask.

Your schedule, hobbies, spare time, food, and sleep change. Of course, interests change also. Our new consuming interest is to be alone with Him! To acquire this treasured time alone with God you will not only release useless, questionable, and bad baggage but also some things that are perfectly legitimate and good. You no longer have time for all the "good things"; you are now making time for the best things!

Expect to be misunderstood by colaborers, other Christians, relatives, friends, and possibly even family. They will think that you have lost interest in them and their personal projects, that you have become quiet and distant. Despite the fact that you "wash your face and dress, as in fasting," you will be perceived as changing. When you attempt to explain, the rumors will be, "he is overdoing it, becoming a little too fanatical." "I don't see why he won't participate or must always leave early." You have not become, nor are you aspiring to be, an eccentric. No, you are simply reordering your life. This will often lead to loss of popularity and to being shunned by others. Popularity and acceptance are so deeply ingrained into us from infancy to the grave, through our dress, activities, and such that it becomes like gold to most. But what is it to gain favor with the world and lose favor with God? We protest, "But I want to try and have both." Ask yourself, "Is that possible? Has it happened in my life?"

Too many of us are being drowned and choked by popularity's heavy gold chains and silver spoons. We must give up "every weight, and the sin that doth so easily beset us" (Heb. 12:1) that we may have God's intimate peace, power, and victory! Your portrait as "Mr. Successful" may be shattered in the ministry, in the church, in the club, in the city. But success before men is no longer your aim but rather obedience before your Master.

In addition to giving up success you can anticipate accelerated assaults by Satan. He understands spiritual warfare. He realizes when a soldier of the cross has moved from basic boot-camp training to advanced individual training in intimacy. Satan realizes full well that the arms, ammunition, and energy to defeat him are found at the feet of Jesus. As you read the Bible you will be reminded that everyone from Abraham to Jesus, and those that followed, experienced accelerated satanic assaults when they set out to know and stand for God. Remember, God has provided all you will ever need to overcome Satan. Why not ask the Lord to provide the energy and armor needed for the assault? Jesus experienced the full price and more for being determined to be about His Father's business.

As you read through these few "costs" and imagine others that might be exacted, it is clear that the world has a tight grip on far too many of us, or we have too tight a grip on the world. If you are struggling, justifying, rationalizing, and trying to explain a less-costly route to the riches of His throne room, then you have found where you are. He waits for you to draw closer. Lay aside any weight that so easily besets you—reach out your hand as did Peter when he was sinking, that He might draw you out and closer so you may know His intimate secrets of walking upon waves of storms.

Prayer

What shall we do once we are alone with Him?

Imagine a young man and woman falling in love. Notice how their actions change. Before they fall in love they hang around their friends, around the church after services. They want to be right in the middle of the crowd, wherever it is. But when love comes, all they have on their mind is getting alone. They talk to each other, they listen to each other. Often they just sit together, walk together, run together. Sometimes they simply look at each other without a motion or word. They usually lose all sense of time. To them, the clock chokes communion. They even have an excessive "hungering and thirsting" to be alone. All of that beautifully pictures our love affair with the Bridegroom of glory! Of course, prayer is the language of a holy love. We shall understand more details of this language later.

Graham Scroggie once commented, "One of the greatest mistakes that a Christian can make is to imagine that social and even spiritual activity can compensate for the lack of sacred communion with God."

George Muller expressed it, "I saw more clearly than ever, that the first and greatest primary business to which I ought to attend to every day was to have my soul happy in the Lord. The first thing to be concerned about was not how much I might serve the Lord but how might I get my soul into a happy state and know the inner life is being nourished by God."

Alan Redpath presses the urgency and tragedy of this matter. "The thing that has marked the failures in my ministry has been the unwillingness to get alone—take time with God—and this has sometimes made me spiritually bankrupt." Isaiah 64:7 speaks to us:

> And there is none that calleth upon thy name, that stirreth up himself to take hold of thee: for thou hast hid they face from us, and hast consumed us, because of our iniquities.

There is something deep in you that says the Lord God Almighty is waiting and wanting a more intimate fellowship. Discover the joys of such a love affair.

May we ourselves not be found somewhere, sometime soon, lost to time but found hungering and thirsting, praying, "Do it again Lord, and let it be in me!"

The Second Essential Element of Intimacy: Obedience

Ye are my friends, if ye do whatsoever I command you (John 15:14).

The words to the song, "Trust and *obey,* for there is no other way," with the added words, "Except to rot and decay," are very true! Obedience is the threshold to spiritual maturity, victory, power, and eternal authority. It is the behavior of our belief, the conduct of our creed, the discipline of our doctrine. Yes, obedience is the very essence of our faith and discipleship.

What use is there to claim we believe if we do not obey? Perhaps a good motto is "No Obey—No Say!"

Graham Scroggie brought the truth home with a dramatic true story. He had finished a tent service and found a young lady in tears, waiting to speak with him. She said, "I truly do want Him to be my Lord, but I'm afraid He might make me a missionary or the like, and I'm afraid to go." Scroggie sat down and opened his Bible to Acts 10:14-15. He began showing her how Peter, when told by the Lord to eat meat which was considered by his Jewish tradition as unclean, argued with the Lord, "Not so, Lord." And the Lord replied to Peter, "What God hath cleansed, that call not thou common."

Scroggie then pointed out this striking truth. It is impossible to say "not so" and "Lord" together. We may say, "Not so," or we may say, "Lord," but not both together. No slave could ever really answer, "Not so, Lord." He is either "Lord," and we obey and say yes, or He is not Lord, and we disobey and say no. The preacher then left the crying girl in the tent with the Bible. Later he returned to find her on her knees over this tear-stained passage. Dr. Scroggie said when he looked over her shoulder, he *saw* her conclusion. She had marked over the words "not so" and was sweetly whispering in prayer, "Yes, Lord, yes, Lord, yes, Lord."

Many Scriptures make it plain that obedience is an essential element of intimacy (see Isa. 1:18-20; John 14:10,15,21,23; 1 John 2:3-6; Heb. 5:9; Prov. 8:34; Jer. 15:16; Ps. 119; Rev. 1:3; Rom. 4:3).

To this I would add a little poem Stephen Olford refers to as his call to obedience.

> Lord, of every thought and
> action

Lord, to send and to stay,
Lord, in writing, speaking, giving
Lord, in all things to *obey.*

Whom Do We Obey?

Why, of course, we obey the Lord! Listen to God's Word:

We ought to obey God rather than man (Acts 5:29).

If I yet pleased men, I should not be the servant of Christ (Gal. 1:10).

Fear him . . . that hath power to cast into hell (Luke 12:4-5).

Have you ever considered all that is implied by Jesus in Luke 11:28? "But he said, Yea rather, blessed are they that hear the word of God, and keep it." The inescapable truth is those that obey Him are pleasing and blessed!

God says in 1 Thessalonians 2:4 that one of the reasons we must obey Him is because He has approved us and trusted us for a special task, and men-pleasing is to have no part. "But as we were allowed of God to be put in trust with the gospel, even so we speak; not as pleasing men, but God, which trieth our hearts."

We read in Ephesians 5:22 and 6:9 God's cycle of submission and its considerable responsibility and rewards. Ephesians 6:10 says we can then depend upon the strength, might, and power of the Lord. These and other passages convince me that the hand of the Lord rests upon those who obey Him. Not to obey the Lord is to "hold hands with Satan" and join his forces of wicked rebellion against God. Rebellion against God's biblical cycle of submission and obedience is certain to bring hindrances to our spiritual well-being. "Likewise, ye husbands, dwell with them according to knowledge, giving honor unto the wife, as unto the weaker vessel, and as being heirs together of the grace of life; that your prayers be not hindered" (1 Pet. 3:7). Since this is true for husbands I believe the same will apply to all those listed in Ephesians 5 and 6. Is it possible that many homes, businesses, children, and others have moved themselves out from under the strength, might, and power of the Lord because of disobedience? I think so!

How Does Obedience Translate in Daily Life?

Caution: At this point we begin to consider the biblical "acid test" of true Christian discipleship. Many will have an urge to draw back here. That is because we have followed the example of so many, so long who have been unwilling to go on with Christ. "Now the just shall live by faith: but if any man draw back, my soul shall have no pleasure in him" (Heb. 10:38). Let us be reminded that we are pushing away from the shores of average Christianity. Don't miss this point! From here on we are not being confronted by some sort of exotic, elite, fanatical, "super-saint" commitment and calling. No! Nothing but normal, biblical Christianity! What may make it seem strange is the fact that our so-called "average" Christianity is somewhat different when compared to normal, basic, reasonable, expected discipleship as demonstrated in the Lord, the apostles, the early church, and the Bible. Thus, the call is back to the "real thing."

> I beseech you therefore, brethren, by the mercies of God, that ye present your bodies a living sacrifice, holy, acceptable unto God, which is your reasonable service. And be not conformed to this world: but be ye transformed by the renewing of your mind, that ye may prove what is that good, and acceptable, and perfect, will of God (Rom. 12:1-2).

While I will write more later about the details of sacrifice, I am now attempting to stress *obedience* as related to sacrifice. Obedience in daily life is our expected and "reasonable service."

In the Old Testament sacrifices were generally within two large categories. There were those for remission of sin and those for thanksgiving. The above passage refers to the sin sacrifice—mercies, etc., done once and for all in Jesus. Then the passage turns to the sort of sacrifice that should go up daily as thanksgiving for our new life in Christ.

The word used in Romans 12:1 for "living sacrifice" is actually *victim*. You may remonstrate now, "But I don't like the idea of victim. I prefer Romans 8:37 where we are referred to as 'more than conquerors.'" Victim and the conqueror coincide "through him that loved us!" We lie down as the victim. He stands up in us as the conqueror! The world sees us as victims to be pitied. God sees us as obedient victors to be praised. Truly, *the way up is down*.

"For whosoever will save his life shall lose it; but whosoever shall lose his life for my sake and the gospel's, the same shall save it" (Mark 8:35). Remember, "Thy Father which seeth in secret himself shall reward thee openly" (6:4).

We are to be a threefold sacrifice. First, we are to be *living sacrifices*. Some boast they are willing to die for Christ, but the call here is not to die but to live for Christ. It may be that, in certain cases, living as a sacrifice is harder than dying as one. I have come to the conclusion that if you are ready to die as a sacrifice you will live as a sacrifice. If you are not now willing to be a living sacrifice, is there any likelihood you would die as a sacrifice for Him? In fact, if we are neither willing to live nor die as a sacrifice, are we ready to die at all?

There are telltale clues to our spiritual whereabouts on this point. I wrote in my notes, "If we are truly willing to crucify ourselves and willing—yea desirous, even to die physically for Christ, then it should be no challenge to rise early for the 'morning watch' (Ps. 63; 2 Cor. 5:6; and 11:27) and to pray for the 'worm work' (Ps. 22) of God's daily grace!"

No challenge at all! If such becomes a great strain, bothersome burden, or struggle, it then becomes all too obvious that we are no longer willing to be the obedient, living sacrifice, which is the very basis of holy intimacy.

The second aspect is that of being a *lasting* sacrifice. The sacrifice of Jesus' life upon the cross for us was a one-time event which never needs repeating. Ah, but our living sacrifice of thanksgiving is exactly the opposite. We are to come again and again and again—day by day by day—over and over and over.

One must be a *lasting* sacrifice and "take up his cross *daily*" (Luke 9:23, author's italics).

My life has been blessed by the daily practice of Bishop Taylor Smith. He said that his first act upon waking in the morning is to present himself a sacrifice unto the Lord. Before rising he says to the Lord, "Lord, I make this bed an altar, and I present my body upon it as a living sacrifice unto You for this day." I too have tried to form that habit, asking God to bathe me, cleanse me, scrub me in the blood of the sacrificed Lamb that I might be a fit sacrifice for the Lamb upon the altar of the day. We are to be living and lasting sacrifices that go daily to the altar. For many, their personal consecration of living has become contaminated because it has been off the altar too long.

You realize, of course, that an altar speaks of suffering and death, even though we might technically live. What is it that will cause you to be such an obedient, sacrificial victim? Where is the pulling power? Where is the appeal of this altar? What could possibly cause you to forever live on "altar avenue"? The answer: it is logical! Third, to be an obedient sacrifice is logical. Daily living as a sacrifice for the believer/servant is but "reasonable service."

In training soldiers for frontline combat there would be a thorough inspection after weeks of intense training. Soldiers would be promised a weekend off for exceptional performance. After the inspection the men would moan and groan upon hearing of their failure, despite the fact they had met all the basic requirements. Then the teaching point was stressed, "Men, to meet the basic requirements is not exceptional performance: it is only your expected, normal, and reasonable service." Many of those men's lives were saved during combat because they had learned what their expected and reasonable service was. By the way, many believers are losing in daily spiritual warfare because they have not learned what their normal and reasonable service is (Luke 17:10).

The word "reasonable" means *logical*. So it is when we look at all Christ has done for us (Rom. 5:6-11).

Some will be called upon to give up job, reputation, popularity, notoriety, family, comfort, even life. Luke 9:45-46 is a picture of so many of us. I wrote in my Bible margin above those verses, "They would not ask about the way of the cross (v. 45), but they were so quick to ask about the crowns." These disciples drew back from the way of sacrifice because of "fear." There is nothing to fear in obeying the Lord. Shadrach, Meshach, and Abed-nego would do nothing but obey their God. They were elevated from living sacrifices up to dying sacrifices for their Lord. "Lo, I see four men loose, walking in the midst of the fire, and they have no hurt; and the form of the fourth is like the Son of God" (Dan. 3:25). They received a presence with the Lord that otherwise was unknown, and the binding ropes put on them by the world of ungodliness were taken away!

The daily life of an obeying and sacrificing servant is one spent in the presence of his Lord with unspeakable freedom by God's power and presence! Don't be afraid of the life of obedient sacrifice!

A person serious about this life of disciplined discipleship is "counting the cost," and undoubtedly asking one of the most important questions possible. "How far will I be asked to follow? How far?"

"All the way my Savior leads me," goes the song. The big question remains, "How far will *I follow Him?*" We are not speaking of salvation but of our earthly lifetime of daily obeying and sacrificing. "How far?"

Abraham's Obedience

Romans 4:2 states, "Abraham believed God." How much? How far?

There are three pivotal events in Abraham's life that clearly serve as examples of obedience for us.

Genesis 12:1: Abraham was called by God to leave his homeland. This was a beautiful place, one of the greatest cities and highly civilized. Abraham was apparently rich and well-to-do in the city. Then the call came! God called him to go and head toward the worst country known at the time, Canaan. He was to be a man with no homeland and to live his life in a nomad's tent.

Only one promise was given. Abraham would produce the offspring that would bless all nations. What would you do? "Abram departed" (v. 4). He left all to obey.

Time passed and Abraham was seventy-five years old, and he and Sara were both "dead" to having children (17:15). The outlook for an offspring to bless the nations was hopeless. What did Abraham do? Romans 4:18 says, "Against all hope Abraham trusted and believed God" (author's words). Twenty-five years later, at the age of one hundred, such trust and obedience was blessed; the baby, Isaac, arrived!

Genesis 22:1-19 chronicles that when Isaac was a youth, God tried and proved Abraham. This was the call for Abraham to sacrifice this long-awaited son. Remember how impossible this call from God must have seemed to Abraham. This was his only son by Sarah. He is the promise, the key, the seed to the Messiah! What would happen if Isaac died? What would Abraham do? He believed and felt that somehow God would not fail him, even if it required a resurrection (Heb. 11:9-17). God honored Abraham's obedience and did provide!

Now what was happening in Abraham's life? God was not punishing, trifling, or stripping one who loved Him. God was proving a man. God had big plans and through obedience He wanted to demonstrate what sort of believer He had.

You can believe that God first intends to see what sort of believer He had in us by our obedience. Expect the test and privilege! Why us? God has gigantic plans. First Thessalonians 2:4 says the gospel is entrusted to us! Do you see how your life parallels Abraham's? We are in on God's master plan, and obedience is the essence of our faith!

The Third Essential Element of Intimacy: The Word
(2 Tim. 3:14-17)

Getting alone with the Lord and obeying Him sound a little novel for most believers today. When we study the Word we know that striving to do this is scriptural. Everything points toward the Word of God. Why would a person be hungering and thirsting? Why would one want to get alone with the Lord? Certainly not to hear the lies of the devil, the call of the world, to dance to the music of the world, to hear the growl of fleshly lust, or to hear the scream of guilt. No, but for one reason, to get alone with the Lord in order to hear a word from God!

What is it that a person would be determined to obey? The answer, of course, is the Word of God! So, then we come to the third essential element of intimacy, the Word of God. To Elijah in 1 Kings 17:2, "The word of the Lord came unto him." Jesus said in Matthew 4:4, "It is written, Man shall not live by bread alone, but by every word that proceedeth out of the mouth of God." When you hear a person preach, teach, and talk, what he says reveals what he knows of the Word of God. But when you hear a person pray and watch him obey and walk, that reveals what he knows of the God of the Word. Vance Havner said, "The Bible is a wonderful book, it comforts the disturbed and it disturbs the comfortable." The Word is essential if we're going to have intimacy with the Lord. It is impossible for me to obey the commands of the Lord if I am not hearing the Commander Himself. Don't forget the idea we are following—to starve the old man and to feed the new man.

My aim when it comes to the Bible, the Word of God, is to empty myself of the trash of this world and to fill myself with the treasures of the Word.

We have said that we are talking about discipline. Well, discipline and the Word will always be related. Those who are growing in the likeness of Christ must be disciplined in the Word of God. How are we to be disciplined? I believe it was Steven Olford who divided up this text under three headings along these lines: verse 14 devoted to the Word, verse 16 directed by the Word, and verse 17 dependent upon the Word. I agree with that outline completely. To be devoted to the Word means we are devoted to continue in the Word and to obey the Word. James said, "Be not hearers only but doers of the Word." In John 14:15, 21, and 23

Jesus says, "If ye love me, keep my commandments. He that hath my commandments, and keepeth them, he it is that loveth me: and he that loveth me shall be loved of my Father, and I will love him, and will manifest myself to him. Jesus answered and said unto him, If a man love me, he will keep my words: and my Father will love him, and we will come unto him, and make our abode with him." "Ye are my friends, if ye do whatsoever I command you" (John 15:14).

When it comes to the Word of God I cannot be "a conscientious objector" any more than I could be a conscientious objector when it comes to my devotion to my family. Never, because there is a devotion to the Word of God in my life. That devotion must go further than lip service while I am on stage. It must go into "life service, backstage." All of this devotion to the Word of God has a great deal to do with my secret duties as a servant.

In John 15:16 we see that it is one thing to be devoted to the Word of God but it is altogether another thing to be directed by the Word of God. In this verse we are given all the ways in which the Word of God helps to direct our life. "But as it is written, Eye hath not seen, nor ear heard, neither have entered into the heart of man, the things which God hath prepared for them that love him. But God hath revealed them unto us by his Spirit: for the Spirit searcheth all things, yea, the deep things of God" (1 Cor. 2:9-10). Also see Psalm 119:9-19.

If we are to become dependent upon the Word of God, we need to ask ourselves a question. What do we want to be for God? We are just as spiritual as we want to be! The Word of God and dependency upon Him are directly related to our spiritual maturity of being "full grown." "The disciple is not above his master: but everyone that is perfect shall be as his master" (Luke 6:40). Dependency upon the Word of God will account for our spiritual activity or "good works." People say, "If I were Billy Graham, if I were Lottie Moon, if I were some famous Christian, I would do thus and such." God knew how to make us and God knew where to put us and if we are devoted to the Word of God—directed by the Word of God, dependent upon the Word of God, alone with the Lord, and obeying Him, we'll be just exactly everything we ought to be. But it is going to take these three essential elements of intimacy for that ever to happen.

Years ago a man told of trying to show off to a rich man. He said, "I stopped a man late at night, who had asked for fifty cents for a cup of coffee. As a self-appointed protector to the rich man I told the beggar to go away. He had about three days growth of beard and he was 'three sheets to the wind.'

"He came back and asked again for fifty cents. This time I shoved him off the sidewalk and he almost went to his knees. In the indignity of that moment his eyes cleared, he looked at me and said, 'I wish you could see the man that I was supposed to be.'"

Friends, I believe the Lord does see us as the man, woman, boy, or girl we are supposed to be! But I'm absolutely convinced that we'll never be that person until, as a believer, we get *alone* with the Lord, we get into the *Word* of God, and we determine to *obey* it. These are the three essential elements of intimacy for the believer!

PART II
The Sacrificed Life Is a
DESIRE

Brethren, I count not myself to have apprehended: but this one thing I do, forgetting those things which are behind, and reaching forth unto those things which are before, I press toward the mark for the prize of the high calling of God in Christ Jesus.   *Philippians 3:13-14*

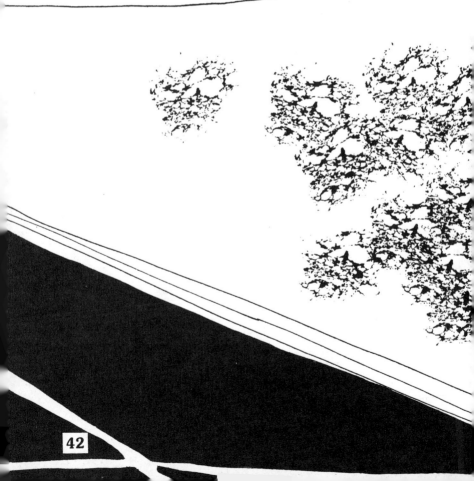

6 | DESIRE AND DISCIPLINE

As I consider my lack of spiritual maturity and my embarrassing number of relapses back into spiritual infancy, I am convicted! My soul is wounded! There is a deep mourning and cry within me to go on in the Lord! Yes—all out after God! Call out, that the heavens may be rent!

My prayer is, "Dear Lord, I crave to go on beyond the glorious introduction of salvation and beyond even knowing You more closely. Oh, my dear Savior, I want to know you intimately, that souls may be rescued from hell, that the world might see in me what kind of people God has—that you, through me, could manifest power, anointing, and victory!"

But how do I go on? How do I grow and mature? I have the spark of desire, but, dear God, give me the *fire!* Oh Lord, fan that fire so it will never go out, and I shall never go back to being content just "inside the door" of "knowing" You! How do you and I grow on in the Lord in such a manner as to keep our hearts ablaze forever?

Feed the New Man

Do you remember the well-worn story about the new convert that came to the missionary who asked him, "How are you doing?" The new convert replied, "I feel like two dogs are fighting inside of me. A good dog and a bad dog." The missionary asked, "Which one is winning?" The new convert came back with, "The dog that I feed the most always wins."

Even though we realize that the Holy Spirit and the new man living within us are not some sort of "dog," the analogy is pointed and profitable to us. We find this to be true in the struggle between the new man and the old man—the winner is always the one that is fed. Therein is the principle of spiritual maturity. It hinges upon feeding and starving! If we feed the new man, and if we starve the old man, then we will find that we will grow in grace, in truth, in the Lord, and in maturity. How do we do that? It seems to me that the mystery lies on two parallel tracks upon which we must go and grow. They are desire and discipline. These two tracks are the two hands in which we receive divine blessing—the two legs upon which we make progress and growth, the two knees upon which we make prayers effectual, the two eyes through which we see spiritual truths, the two ears through which we understand the voice and will of God, the two lips through which we convincingly declare the gospel. We feed the new man and starve the old man by moving upon the tracks of desire and discipline.

Desire and discipline are like Siamese twins that do not look exactly alike but are inseparable. If you try to separate one from the other you will have spiritual abnormality or deformity and eventually spiritual stifling to the hope of any substantial growth and intimacy. With God it is more than "let go and let God."

It must be both trust and obey—desire and discipline! Our spiritual vehicle makes progress toward maturity along these two parallel tracks, the weight needing to be equally distributed upon each track. If we lean too heavily on the track named desire we will end up being wild-eyed, emotional fanatics drowning in our own froth. If we lean too heavily only upon discipline, we end up being dried-out, prune-faced, legalistic, spiritual deadheads. No, it is both, wide and deep, demanding and dependable, desire and discipline.

Philippians 4:8: "Finally, brethren, whatsoever things are true, whatsoever things are honest, whatsoever things are just, whatsoever things are pure, whatsoever things are lovely, whatsoever things are of good report; if there be any virtue, and if there be any praise, think on these things."

Take a look at the old man within you! Is he robbing, killing, ruining, mocking everything good and holy about you? Do not stand for it! Determine now that you are going to starve him down to practical nonexistence. This is a diet that is extremely demanding, but God is especially interested in helping us follow through on it!

Discipline is an ugly word to many people, but it is not just a negative: it is also an avenue of spiritual benefits. Discipline is the rule of life. You look into sports, in music, in business. Those who have done well have practiced discipline.

No, I am not calling for surrender of your will. No, not at all. I'm calling for you to exercise your will! There's been so much talk about surrender that we have become spiritually soft and soggy, surrendering all to everyone at anytime. There is, of course, a place for surrender to the Lord, but there is still a place for willful determination. This is a time to exercise one's will. Joshua 14:15 says, "Choose you this day whom ye will serve," or may I paraphrase that to "Whom you shall feed"? Psalm 37:5 says, "Commit; . . . trust, . . . and [expect]." Such is an exercise of the will. All hangs on this. Will you decide now to starve down the old man?"

Is this too intense, too strong, too aggressive, too militant? No, it is not! I, like thousands of other pastors, am a heart doctor fresh from the operating room of daily life—battling, digging, cutting, scraping, fighting, giving heart-to-heart resuscitation. We are trying to enliven Christians that have lost the will to discipline their lives and therefore have lost the spiritual victory upon the daily battlefield.

Somebody will say, "What happened to those people that failed to stand in the victory?" Simply this, they never exercised spiritual discipline. They took the route of least resistance. They allowed the old man to be fed by the world's system and the new man shriveled up, while the old man rose up! There must be discipline. Trust and obey for there's no other way—except to rot and decay!

But before there will be discipline in our lives there must be a desire, a desire to follow intimacy with God.

7 | FOLLOWING PASSIONATELY AFTER GOD

Oh God, thou art my God, early will I seek thee: my soul thirsteth for thee, my flesh longeth for thee in a dry and thirsty land, where no water is; To see thy power and thy glory, so as I have seen thee in the sanctuary. Because thy loving-kindness is better than life, my lips shall praise thee. Thus will I bless thee while I live: I will lift up my hands in thy name. My soul shall be satisfied as with marrow and fatness; and my mouth shall praise thee with joyful lips: When I remember thee upon my bed, and meditate on thee in the night watches. Because thou hast been my help, therefore in the shadow of thy wings will I rejoice. My soul followeth hard after thee: thy right hand upholdeth me (Ps. 63:1-8).

Hear my cry, O God; attend unto my prayer. From the end of the earth will I cry unto thee, when my heart is overwhelmed lead me to the rock that is higher than I (Ps. 61:1-2).

As the hart panteth after the water brooks, so panteth my soul after thee, O God. My soul thirsteth for God, for the living God: when shall I come and appear before God? (Ps. 42:1-2).

My soul longeth, yea, even fainteth for the courts of the Lord: my heart and my flesh crieth out for the living God (Ps. 84:2).

I stretch forth my hands unto thee: my soul thirsteth after thee, as a thirsty land (Ps. 143:6).

There is a great deal of difference in knowing the Word of God and knowing the God of the Word. David, like Daniel and many others, was of "the people that do know their God shall be strong, and do exploits" (Dan. 11:32). David was a man "*after*

48

God's own heart" (see 1 Sam. 13:14; Acts 13:22). He knew God as well as the Word of God.

Some have commented that we are just as spiritual as we want to be, and we don't have revival because we are content to live without it. Ian Thomas said, "All there is of God is available to those who are available to all there is of God." This is illustrated by the combustion engine. The combustion engine was not only invented to demonstrate its parts moving, but it was invented to demonstrate the inherent capacity of a new substance which had been discovered, oil. The engine was developed so the oil could be used.

Likewise, God created man, not to demonstrate an inherent capacity for man to do something, but only that God may be released in and through that man. That is exactly why God created us, not to see us do anything, but that He might be released through us. That is only going to happen when we become intimately close to Him (God has no favorites, but God does have intimates), and we will realize that intimacy only when we are following hard after Him.

Leonard Ravenhill gives the illustration of a junk car. Suppose a man buys a junk car that will not run. He brings it home, scrapes all the rust off, cleans all the gunk off the engine, takes all the dirt and mud off. Suppose the man then takes all that trash into the house and puts it before his family and says, "Look what I bought for $500." The family would think he was crazy to have bought all that junk, dirt, mud, and gunk! They would be correct.

However, the man really bought the automobile, not for all that junk and mud and gunk that came with it, but for the automobile itself. Since the man owns it, that automobile will represent this man's character and who he is. The man will want the automobile to be clean, in good repair, and in the very best condition because wherever it is seen or wherever it is parked or wherever it is used, it will be a reflection of its owner. This is precisely what God did with us when He saved us through Jesus. He did not save us to keep all of our sin and all of the stain and all the ugliness—not at all! He saved us in order to clean us up and to reflect Himself through us wherever we go and whatever we do.

> Who gave himself for us, that he might redeem us from all iniquity, and purify unto himself a peculiar people, zealous of good works (Titus 2:14).

> And that he died for all, that they which live should not henceforth live unto themselves, but unto him which died for them and rose again (2 Cor. 5:15).

God wants unlimited access to you. He wants to teach your mind. He wants to control your emotions. He wants to direct your will. He wants to govern your behavior. Why? So when people see you they may know who God really is!

> In whom ye also are builded together for an habitation of God through the Spirit (Eph. 2:22).

We are to be the habitation of God. Consequently God will supply all of our needs just like He said (Phil. 4:19), but God is not going to push the cart and be the bag boy! We, the church, need to get under the travail, the agony, and the discipline of following hard after God!

There is a price to be paid for spiritual power and progress. Believers cannot simply jump up and start killing giants like David did Goliath. So many times we fail to see the great truth that lies behind spiritual "giant-killing."

> And Saul said to David, Thou art not able to go against this Philistine to fight with him: for thou art but a youth, and he a man of war from his youth. And David said unto Saul, Thy servant kept his father's sheep, and there came a lion, and a bear, and took a lamb out of the flock: And I went out after him, and smote him, and delivered it out of his mouth: and when he arose against me, I caught him by his beard, and smote him, and slew him. Thy servant slew both the lion and the bear: and this uncircumcised Philistine shall be as one of them, seeing he hath defied the armies of the living God. David said moreover, The Lord that delivered me out of the paw of the lion, and out of the paw of the bear, he will deliver me out of the hand of this Philis-

tine. And Saul said unto David, Go, and the Lord be with thee
(1 Sam. 17:33-37).

We are aware that before David confronted Goliath he had
first killed a lion and a bear. You see, he was working up to
giants. He had found out, alone with only the Lord in the wilderness, that God was able. By paying the price of being alone with
the Lord and facing difficulty after difficulty with confidence in
God, he was then able to overcome the giant that stood against
him. This same situation is true in our own spiritual warfare. So
many of us are unable even to eliminate spiritual mice, rats, and
rabbits. We've not be willing to pay the price to be alone with God
in preparation for spiritual giant-killing. What's wrong with us?
We're like Peter in Matthew 26:58, we follow "afar off," or Ephesians 2:13, "But now in Christ Jesus ye who sometimes were far
off are made nigh by the blood of Christ." What do we need to
do? Friend, we need to become one of God's intimates!

In my diary I wrote this prayer right after the Lord broke my
heart on this point. "Lord, I want with all my heart to be lost in
Your love, in Your will, in Your hand. Seal me in, dear Lord
Jesus! Lock the door, throw away the key, seal the door completely that I may never ever escape! If I should hear the call of
anything outside, please, Lord Jesus, sing the song of victory so
loudly that I may hear only You. If I should close my foolish ears
even to such a song and go for the door, please put an angel as at
the garden of Eden, strong and mighty, to stop my move. And if
by some means I should pass the angel and begin to beg, plead,
cry, and claw at the door—please, please, please, dear Lord,
allow no man, or power, or principality, or force of this or any
other world to be able to lure me with any slightest hope of es-
caping my lostness in Your love, will, and hand!

"Father, catch me in the runaway current of You, flood me and
wash me and soak me, in an irreversible style, with Your love,
will, and hand!

"Dear Jesus, may my lostness in Your love be so real that it
may call those without to within rather than those not within calling me out! May this be so for Your glory and my growing."

Not as though I had already attained, either were already perfect: but I follow after, if that I may apprehend that for which also I am apprehended of Christ Jesus (Phil. 3:12).

Then said Jesus unto his disciples, If any man will come after me, let him deny himself, and take up his cross, and follow me (Matt. 16:24).

That the righteousness of the law might be fulfilled in us, who walk not after the flesh, but after the Spirit. For they that are after the flesh do mind the things of the flesh; but they that are after the Spirit the things of the Spirit (Rom. 8:4-5).

Blessed are they which do hunger and thirst after righteousness: for they shall be filled (Matt. 5:6).

When we read in Luke 8:43-48 and Matthew 9:20-23 about the woman with the issue of blood, we note those words that indicate the place of power—she fell down. That's the place of power, down near the feet of Jesus. Look at Zacchaeus in the tree, at Joshua concerned over his house. Job said, "Though he slay me, yet will I trust in him" (Job 13:15). Peter was saying, "Though I drown, I'm going to follow Him." Daniel was saying, "Though the lions may eat me, I will follow Him." Shadrach, Meshach, and Abed-nego were saying, "Though we may burn, we will follow Him." Hallelujah, none did. Not one was lost! Each found the holy intimacy of God's presence! Look in the tree, in the furnace, in the lions' den, in the sea, in Job's house, in the crowd. All found the holy presence of God!

The Pharisees heard that the people murmured such things concerning him; and the Pharisees and the chief priests sent officers to take him. Then said Jesus unto them, Yet a little while am I with you, and then I go unto him that sent me. Ye shall seek me, and shall not find me: and where I am, thither ye cannot come. Then said the Jews among themselves, Whither will he go, that we shall not find him? Will he go unto the dispersed among the Gentiles and teach the Gentiles? What manner of saying is this that he said, ye shall seek me, and shall not find me: and where I am, thither ye cannot come? In the last day, that great day of the feast, Jesus stood and cried, saying, If any man thirst, let him come unto me, and drink (John 7:32-37).

Let us be honest here. Perhaps we have talked too much about "God is waiting." God is ready when you are. God has not left you; you have left Him. Anytime you are ready—God is ready. Maybe it's time we remember, "Seek ye the Lord while he may be found" (Isa. 55:6).

Dear Lord, may we be found following intimately and closely after You.

8 | "THAT THOU WOULDEST REND THE HEAVENS"

If most of us are going to move on from where we are spiritually and follow hard after God, we must desperately have a desire for help from heaven! After all, haven't we tried again and again to resolve, to commit, to rededicate, only to make another "false start" and fall flat on our faces into the same old pattern of spiritual numbness?

Even now as our hearts jump again with even the smallest hope of a new try, the devil whispers, "What's the use? It'll be the same as before. Not long, and you'll be right back on your face in the dirt. You're not going anywhere, and besides all this, just look around at the others. You're not so bad!" Frankly there really is little hope, unless we receive help from heaven! Dear God, our earnest desire is that Thou wouldest rend heaven and help us!

Oh, that thou wouldest rend the heavens, that thou wouldest come down, that the mountains might flow down at thy presence. As when the melting fire burneth, the fire causeth the waters to boil, to make thy name known to thine adversaries, that the nations may tremble at thy presence! When thou didst terrible things which we looked not for, thou camest down, the mountains flowed down at thy presence. For since the beginning of the world men have not heard, nor perceived by the ear, neither hath the eye seen, O God, beside thee, what he hath prepared for him that waiteth for him. Thou meetest him that rejoiceth and worketh righteousness, those that remember thee in thy ways: behold, thou art wroth; for we have sinned: in those is continuance, and we shall be saved. But we are all as an unclean thing, and all our righteousnesses are as filthy rags; and we all do fade as a leaf; and our iniquities, like the wind, have taken us away. And there is none that calleth upon thy name, that stirreth up himself to take hold of thee: for thou hast hid thy face from us, and hast consumed us, because of our iniquities. But now, O Lord, thou art our father; we are the clay, and thou our potter; and we all are the work of thy hand. Be not wroth very sore, O Lord, neither remember iniquity forever: behold, see, we beseech thee, we are all thy people. Thy holy cities are a wilderness, Zion is a wilderness, Jerusalem a desolation. Our holy and our beautiful house, where our fathers praised thee, is burned up with fire: and all our pleasant things are laid waste. Wilt thou refrain thyself for these things, O Lord? wilt thou hold thy peace, and afflict us very sore? (Isa. 64:1-12).

The background of this passage of Scripture is that the nation of Israel had sinned. God had punished the people by allowing them to receive what they deserved. Now they saw their trouble, and Isaiah was sent by God to call out for them. Isaiah and Israel were pictures of the church and the believer today and what we should do in order that heaven might be opened and God may come down and give us help. The nation of Israel had entered into and was suffering physical slavery. Today the church suffers from missing God's best and God's power. It suffers from compromise, impotence, moral decay, and spiritual blindness, all of which is the result of not maturing in the Lord.

A. W. Rainsbury, in a message, really impressed my heart with a three-word outline around which I've had some earnest thinking in hopes that heaven might be rent. The following are some thoughts on those three words—a *cry,* a *confession,* and a *covenant.*

A Cry

In verses 1-5 of Isaiah 64, a cry for God's intervention goes up. Everything in America seems to be broken. Our cities are broken, our economy, marriages, families, lives, peace. It seems that everything in America is broken *except* the hearts of the believers and the church!

"Oh," was the cry that opened the windows to man's hurt, his deep grief, his desperate longing. If we are to see heaven move, we must first move ourselves. There must be some heart-brokenness, some unutterable longing for God to come down and help us. "Oh God, look down, rend heaven, come down, help us!" (author's words). Some way we must have in our souls the plea of the nobleman when he cried, "Come down ere my child die."

This was a cry for a movement of God, a cry for meeting with the power of God. We do not need a regular Sunday morning meeting: we need a mountain-melting meeting. Our need is not for more "softly-and tenderly" tugging—we need an earthquake. We need to exchange a candlelight service for one that will set the world on fire and boil spiritually stagnant waters! "Come down, dear Lord, burn out the dross. Set our souls afire in love and zeal!" Why, to fill our churches, to make us happy, to see great miracles? No. The answer comes in verse 2, "To make thy name known to thine adversaries"—to vindicate the character of God before the mocking, blasphemous world, that the world may have the experience that verse 5 indicates—that they have never seen a God like our God! We must remember this sort of manifestation of God is not just casually handed out. As Jesus said, "These things cometh by prayer and fasting." There are conditions: "Prepared for those that waiteth for him." That's exactly what 1 Corinthians 2:9-10 is talking about. This is not speaking about heaven and the hereafter, for it's talking about treasures for the believer that are promised and provided for *here* and *now*. Waiting means more than sitting around. It means loving and living and obeying and trusting. Make no mistake about it, God never provides divine treasures and a human key. No, the key is also divine as well. Those divine treasures are the deep things of God. Every believer can have them with Him in His fullness.

A Confession

After the cry there comes a confession of sin, "Behold, thou art wroth; for we have sinned" (v. 5). Here is humility and honesty. Humility: "We" are all in this together, says the prophet of God. Someone might say, "Well, preacher, all will never get right at the same time!" If we do not we will never see God move like He wants. The truth is *we could if we would!*

The honesty: "for our sins." This wasn't an immediate, recent, incidental, and accidental sin. The depth and duration of the sin are indicated in four figures—the leper who is unclean, the pollution of the garment, the leaf that has fallen to the ground, and the wind which depict how sin can take us so far away. The worst facet about the sin is in verse 7. No one calls upon God, no one stirs themselves, and no one is taking hold of God. This sort of attitude and smugness of God's people rendered a bad effect upon themselves, but it had a worse effect upon God. God then let them suffer the consequences of their sin.

Judges 16:20 tells of Samson, when the power of God had departed from him and "he wist not." I also think of 1 Samuel 4:21 when the name "Ichabod" was given to Eli's grandson, because the glory of God had departed from Israel. Perhaps we need to press the urgency of making our move toward the Lord, even as believers, calling on Him and confessing Him!

A Covenant

The third aspect of this appeal, that was designed by God to rend heaven, was: it was to be a covenant appeal (v. 8). There are three names given in this verse all of which appeal to their relationship to God, Father, Potter, and Creator. Truly His name is wonderful! His name is but a picture of His awesome character. Here is a picture of God's people coming to themselves, waking up, and remembering who they are and who their God really is! Ezra 1:1 said God came down! How true that has always been when God's people cry out for heaven to be rent, confessing their sins, and making that covenant appeal as His children. That's the hope and help we need to move on in the fullness of Christ. Will we make this our heartfelt desire?

Warning: If the Spirit of God is now bringing you to this point of earnest desire to follow hard after God in an intimate fellowship, you must remember that it is *the sacrificed life* which is ahead for your life. However, before any of us enter upon or make any worthwhile distance upon *the sacrificed life* we must make our great escape from the prison house of prosperity.

Caution: This prison house has an extremely subtle security system which enables it to keep its prisoners in bondage even while they are feeling and declaring they are free!

9 | THE SACRIFICED LIFE (THE FOOLISH WAY) EXAMINED

For the grace of God that bringeth salvation hath appeared to all men, Teaching us that, denying ungodliness and worldly lusts, we should live soberly, . . . Looking for that blessed hope, and the glorious appearing of the great God and our Savior Jesus Christ; Who gave himself for us, that he might redeem us from all iniquity, and purify unto himself a peculiar people, zealous of good works. These things speak, and exhort, and rebuke with all authority. Let no man despise thee (Titus 2:11-15).

A Peculiar People

A fool is defined as one who does not appear to have good sense. The Bible speaks directly about and to the fool (Prov. 17:24-25; 18:2,6-7; 19:13, 20:3; 26:3-4). Jesus in Matthew 5:22 said, "Whosoever shall say, Thou fool, shall be in danger of hell fire." But in light of all the above I am still willing to say that to follow Christ is "the way of a fool." Jesus said in John 14:6, "I am the way." What way? The Sacrificed Life! Are you asking us to make fools of ourselves to sacrifice our lives? No, but we need to know that if we follow Christ intimately, the world will see to it that we are called fools. The truth of life is that in God's sight, fools are those that are spiritually ignorant, uninformed, and follow after the ways of the world. "But God said unto him, Thou fool, this night thy soul shall be required of thee: then whose shall those things be, which thou hast provided?" (Luke 12:20). Conversely, in the world's sight, fools are those who follow after the way of Christ. "Jesus answered, My kingdom is not of this world: if my kingdom were of this world, then would my servants fight, that I should not be delivered to the Jews: but now is my kingdom not from hence" (John 18:36).

Whose Fool Are You?

Our pride argues, "I don't want to be a fool at all! I want to be a nice, balanced, practical person in the sight of the world and in the sight of God." However, there are two major problems with this approach to life for the believer. First, that sort of life is certain to bring compromise with the world. Next, Jesus makes it plain that a believer cannot serve two masters. He will hate one and love the other.

The "sacrificed life" in following Christ is critical. These truths are foundational for all that is essential in mature spiritual living. Such truths we will discover are essential for greatness in heaven throughout eternity. We can expect the old man to recoil "naturally" and draw back from this foolish way as we come to understand more about it. "Now the just shall live by faith: but if any man draw back, my soul shall have no pleasure in him" (Heb. 10:38). All flesh automatically avoids crucifixion!

Every believer faces a choice. One might ask, "Why can't I just go on as I am?" You certainly may; in fact, most do. But the pressing question is: "What is the Holy Spirit calling and asking of you right now?" The foolish way is precisely what Jesus was clarifying with the twelve apostles in Matthew 20:24-25, "You know the way of the earthly rulers. Well, our way is exactly the opposite" (author's words). Hence, our way will seem foolish to the world and even to Christians who are worldly minded. "There is a way which seemeth right unto a man, but the end thereof are the ways of death" (Prov. 14:12). The way of the world moves forward on politics, manipulation, influence, self-seeking, self-promoting, charm, and personality. The way of the world is foolish to God and to those who are spiritual but seems wise to worldly minded people. The way of the *Word* is foolish to the world but is wisdom to God and to those who are spiritually minded.

Here I list several things that make the way of the Christian life seem foolish.

(1) Following Christ Will Seem to be "The Foolish Way"

"Let no man deceive himself. If any man among you seemeth to be wise in this world, let him become a fool, that he may be wise. For wisdom of this world is foolishness with God" (1 Cor. 3:18-19).

(2) Telling People About the Cross of Christ Will Be Deemed "Foolish"

Personal witnessing is deemed particularly peculiar. "And as he thus spake for himself, Festus said with a loud voice, Paul, thou art beside thyself; much learning doth make thee mad. But he said, I am not mad, most noble Festus; but speak forth the words of truth and soberness" (Acts 26:24-25).

(3) Faith Living Appears to Be "The Foolish Way"

"As you have therefore received Christ Jesus the Lord, so walk ye in him" (Col. 2:6). We have received the Lord by faith and therefore we are to walk by faith (Hab. 2:4; Rom. 1:17; Gal. 3:11; Heb. 10:38; Rom. 10:17).

(4) Nonconformity Is "The Foolish Way"

"And be not conformed to this world: but be ye transformed by the renewing of your mind, that ye may prove what is that good, and acceptable, and perfect, will of God" (Rom. 12:2). The world rewards conformity and penalizes nonconformity. You can see this in school as well as at work. However, when it comes to the spiritual life, God rewards nonconformity and penalizes conformity to the world. The world thrives on popularity which is gained by acceptance, and that is governed by what the majority thinks. If you are transformed you should not conform. Therefore, you will be called foolish. In light of the fact that we will always be called fools by the majority makes us remember that there is a broad way and many there be that are headed for destruction. And there is a narrow way and few are on it. (In fact, the way will seem narrower for those who are following more closely after Christ.)

(5) *The Message of the Cross Seems "Foolish"*

The world has confidence in the flesh and humanity. The message of the cross is "a stumbling block" (a "scandal") and "foolishness" to many who consider themselves philosophical and intellectual. Man is looking for something acceptable, agreeable, undisturbing, and unchanging. We must admit that the cross is radical! Humanism teaches that we can get better and better. The message of the cross is exactly the opposite, and the world calls it foolishness.

Hell is not solely populated by "bad" people. Many "good" people are in hell simply because they did not think they were bad enough to go. If you follow the way of the cross you are indeed on *the foolish way*. This is exactly how the great apostle Paul was perceived in Acts 17:32 by the mocking Mars Hill crowd. "And when they heard of the resurrection of the dead, some mocked: and others said, We will hear again of this matter." That is exactly how the world viewed Jesus the day He died on the cross. And it is going to be the same when we follow His way, whether at school, at work, or even in our families.

(6) *Wanting Nothing but Jesus Will Make You Appear on "The Foolish Way"*

"But what things were gain to me, those I counted loss for Christ. Yea doubtless, and I count all things but loss for the excellency of the knowledge of Christ Jesus my Lord: for whom I have suffered the loss of all things, and do count them but dung, that I may win Christ. And be found in him, not having mine own righteousness, which is of the law, but that which is through the faith of Christ, the righteousness which is of God by faith: That I may know him, and the power of his resurrection, and the fellowship of his sufferings, being made conformable unto his death; If by any means I might attain unto the resurrection of the dead" (Phil. 3:7-11).

"For I determined not to know anything among you, save Jesus Christ, and him crucified" (1 Cor. 2:2).

"But the natural man receiveth not the things of the Spirit of God: for they are foolishness unto him: neither can he know them, because they are spiritually discerned" (1 Cor. 2:14).

(7) Giving Your Money Is Seen as "The Foolish Way"

"Bring ye all the tithes into the storehouse, that there may be meat in mine house, and prove me now herewith, saith the Lord of hosts, if I will not open you the windows of heaven, and pour you out a blessing, that there shall not be room enough to receive it" (Mal. 3:10).

"Give, and it shall be given unto you; good measure, pressed down, and shaken together, and running over, shall men give into your bosom. For with the same measure that ye mete withal it shall be measured to you again" (Luke 6:38).

If a believer really follows the biblical principles of financial stewardship he will undoubtedly be considered foolish by the world. How many times have we believers completely baffled our associates and friends, and even family, by our desire to follow these truths, knowing full well they felt we were being foolish with our money?

(8) Endeavoring to Live the Spirit-Controlled Life Will Seem "Foolish"

"For these are not drunken, as ye suppose, seeing it is but the third hour of the day" (Acts 2:15).

To seek God's leadership in everything and allowing Him to dictate our every move is indeed a strange life in the eyes of the world.

(9) Giving Up the Worldly Life Comes Across as "The Foolish Way" to Those Caught by the World (Matt. 16:21-27).

"Whosoever will come after me, let him deny himself, and take up his cross, and follow me" (Mark 8:34; also see Luke 9:23).

"For what shall it profit a man, if he shall gain the whole world and lose his own soul?" (Mark 8:36).

"The hour is come, that the Son of man should be glorified. Verily, verily, I say unto you, Except a corn of wheat fall into the ground and die, it abideth alone: but if it die, it bringeth forth much fruit. He that loveth his life shall lose it; and he that hateth his life in this world shall keep it unto life eternal. If any man serve me, let him follow me; and where I am, there shall also my servant be: if any man serve me, him will my Father honor" (John 12:23-26).

(10) Humility Is "The Foolish Way" to the World Which Is Built Upon and Motivated by Pride

"Whosoever therefore shall humble himself as this little child, the same is greatest in the kingdom of heaven" (Matt. 18:4).

The humble life is the life that pleases the Lord as illustrated in Luke 14:7-11 and 18:9-14. "And he said unto them, Ye are they which justify yourselves before men; but God knoweth your hearts: for that which is highly esteemed among men is abomination in the sight of God" (Luke 16:15).

(11) To Starve the Old Man Seems "Foolish"

To "starve" the old man and "feed" the new man within the believer will seem utter foolishness to the world whose philosophy is "eat, drink, and be merry, for tomorrow you may die."

Paul is seen as a fool because of this very approach to the "old man" (Acts 17:18-19).

(12) Lack of Concern for Worldly Comforts Will Be Considered "The Foolish Way"

"Carry neither purse, nor scrip, nor shoes: and salute no man by the way" (Luke 10:4).

"And Jesus saith unto him, The foxes have holes, and the birds of the air have nests; but the Son of man hath not where to lay his head" (Matt. 8:20).

"Provide neither gold, nor silver, nor brass in your purses, Nor scrip for your journey, neither two coats, neither shoes, nor yet staves: for the workman is worthy of his meat" (Matt. 10:9-10; see 2 Tim. 4:10).

(13) Seeking to Serve Will be Considered "The Foolish Way"

"Even as the Son of man came not to be ministered unto, but to minister, and to give his life a ransom for many" (Matt. 20:28).

The servant life is contrary to the world's attitude as reflected in J. B. Phillips's play on the Beatitudes:

Happy are the "pushers": for they get on in the world.
Happy are the hardboiled: for they never let life hurt them.
Happy are they who complain: for they get their way in the end.
Happy are the blasé: for they never worry over their sins.
Happy are the slave drivers: for they get results.
Happy are the knowledgeable men of the world: for they know their way around.

To live contrary to the world's attitudes is interpreted as the foolish way. The most foolish goal possible, from the world's view, is to desire the life of a servant/intercessor.

All of these thirteen reasons and many others will be considered as foolish ways to those who do not view life through spiritual eyes—but in fact this is really the "narrow way" upon which a servant is to travel.

But Why Would Anyone Want to Be on Such a Foolish Way?

(1) When we took Christ as our Savior we bargained to follow a servant! Jesus had an opportunity in the wilderness, as He confronted Satan, to make His progress by jumping off a tower and amazing everyone. But instead of jumping from a tower, Jesus took up a towel and the life of a servant/intercessor. Christians are constantly faced with the choice of a tower or a towel.

(2) We are seeking to be conformed to His image and therefore are compelled to follow the servant life.

(3) Jesus lives in us and He yearns to be Himself (a servant/intercessor) on what seems to be a foolish way! Christ changed when He entered you no more than you changed when you put on a different set of clothes. "Jesus Christ the same yesterday, and today, and forever" (Heb. 13:8).

(4) We see with spiritual eyes: therefore we recognize the value of the servant life and the foolish way. In the terms of Ephesians 6:17 our "helmet" is correctly adjusted! "Now faith is the substance of things hoped for, the evidence of things not seen" (Heb. 11:1).

(5) Pleasing our Father leads us to follow this path. "For this is the will of God, even your sanctification" (1 Thess. 4:3).

(6) The way to eternal greatness follows a path that seems foolish (Matt. 20:26). Do not trade temporal, momentary greatness for eternal greatness!

To paraphrase a statement I heard somewhere, it is a well-known fact: when the devil finds that his fiery darts fall away harmless from us, the feather-light arrow of a sarcastic smile which says, "You look so foolish living such a life," will often kill the progress of a believer attempting to live the servant life. There is only one way to combat such confrontation, and that is to go on quietly and peacefully as an obedient servant, following the light your Master has so graciously given you.

Let us be of good cheer when we are declared on the foolish way for so they labeled Jesus (John 10:20; Mark 3:21), Rhoda

(Acts 12:15), and Paul the apostle throughout Acts and Romans.

"Better a thousand times effective peculiarity than ineffective ordinariness."

Conclude now that what may seem to be foolish is the only true way for a Christian to live. Desire this way!

Read the following verses carefully in order that you might have confidence along the foolish way as a servant of the King.

> I am become a fool in glorying; ye have compelled me: for I ought to have been commended of you: for in nothing am I behind the very chiefest apostles, though I be nothing (2 Cor. 12:11). And I was with you in weakness, and in fear, and in much trembling. And my speech and my preaching was not with enticing words of man's wisdom, but in demonstration of the Spirit and of power: That your faith should not stand in the wisdom of men, but in the power of God" (1 Cor. 2:3-5).

> And let us consider one another to provoke unto love and to good works (Heb. 10:24).

> But we were gentle among you, even as a nurse cherisheth her children: So being affectionately desirous of you, we were willing to have imparted unto you, not the gospel of God only, but also our own souls, because ye were dear unto us (1 Thess. 2:7-8).

> Wherefore comfort yourselves together, and edify one another, even as also ye do (1 Thess. 5:11).

> For, brethren, ye have been called unto liberty; only use not liberty for an occasion to the flesh, but by love serve one another (Gal 5:13).

> For the love of Christ constraineth us; because we thus judge, that if one died for all, then were all dead: And that he died for all, that they which live should not henceforth live unto themselves, but unto them which died for them, and rose again (2 Cor. 5:14-15).

> For we preach not ourselves, but Christ Jesus the Lord; and ourselves your servants for Jesus' sake (2 Cor. 4:5).

> Be kindly affectioned one to another with brotherly love; in honor preferring one another; Not slothful in business; fervent in

spirit; serving the Lord; Rejoicing in hope; patient in tribulation, continuing instant in prayer; Distributing to the necessity of saints; given to hospitality (Rom. 12:10-13).

Wherefore be ye not unwise, but understanding what the will of the Lord is (Eph. 5:17).

Indeed we desire this foolish way because the "love of Christ constrains us," but our desire is also stirred by a startling, chilling, and provocative statement—"No Equality in Heaven."

10 | NO EQUALITY IN HEAVEN*

Whosoever therefore shall break one of these *least* commandments, and shall teach men so, he shall be called the *least* in the kingdom of heaven: but whosoever shall do and teach them, the same shall be called *great* in the kingdom of heaven (Matt. 5:19, author's italics).

Whosoever therefore shall humble himself as this little child, the same is *greatest* in the kingdom of heaven (Matt. 18:4, author's italics).

But it shall not be so among you: but whosoever will be *great* among you, let him be your minister; And whosoever will be *chief* among you, let him be your servant: (Matt. 20:26-27, author's italics).

"No Equality in Heaven" is a provocative phrase. But that is exactly what the above texts are pointing us toward. If the believer accepts "No Equality in Heaven" as true, then he faces some serious questions and usually some very drastic life changes. This statement means that "things" are not the same for everyone who goes to heaven. We want to draw back from this statement that seems incomprehensible to us. Most of us have been led to believe just the opposite, that things are, in fact, the same for everyone in heaven. It is easier and simpler to believe

---

*Important Notation: Of course not everyone will quickly agree with all the following conclusions of "No Equality in Heaven." However, no one can disagree that the Bible and the life of Jesus teach us that God wants His followers to live the servant/ intercessor life patterns after His Son. Therefore, regardless of a person's view of last things, all believers must conclude that for them to live the Christ life is for them to live the servant life while here on earth.

that things are the same for all who enter heaven. If we believe there is no equality in heaven we must then face the fact that God has some heavenly desires for the believer's earthly living, after salvation, which have eternal consequences.

I have found that deep in most believers' hearts there is a witness within to this truth of no equality in heaven. Does that witness within you say yes or no to the following questions.

(1) We agree that the thief on the cross and the apostle Paul both went to heaven. However, does it seem true that a man who had spent his life away from God in sin and comes to the Lord at the last minute would receive the same inheritance as one who gave his life in such unparalleled commitment as did the apostle Paul?

(2) Consider a rapist and murderer who receives Christ on death row, moments before his execution. Compare such a man to one who receives Christ at nine years of age, lives his life clean, holy, and separated and gives his entire life in meritorious service on the mission field to the glory of God.

Now the questions:—Is it true that the thief on the cross receives the same inheritance throughout all eternity as did Paul? Is it true that the death row man receives the same inheritance throughout all eternity as the missionary? Isn't there a witness inside of us that wants to respond to these two questions with "No"? "No, they are not equal in eternity." Understand very clearly that this subject is in no way suggesting there are different degrees in salvation. That would be heresy! No, this subject deals with differences in rewards after the saved are in heaven.

It is clear that there is eternal inheritance for all true Christian believers (Eph. 1:11,14, Col. 1:12; 3:24, Heb. 6:9-12; Rom. 4:13, 16-17; 1 Pet. 1:3-5; and 1 Cor. 3:21-23). All believers (the saved thief, Paul, the murderer, the missionary) will undoubtedly be equal in receiving eternal life, righteousness, perfection, glorified bodies, presence of the Trinity, and joy, as well as those things listed in Revelation 21:4, "And God shall wipe away all tears from their eyes; and there shall be no more death, neither sorrow, nor crying, neither shall there be any more pain:

for the former things are passed away," and surely even much more! I would term these as "general" eternal inheritances and blessings. These are shared equally by all believers. What a thrill for all believers to spend all eternity in such splendid fashion! But isn't there more?

Upon examining Matthew 5:19; 18:4; 20:26-27, along with other passages, one begins to see shades of something more in eternity than the "general" blessings. There appear to be things *not* equally inherited and shared by all believers. "He whose work is burned down shall forfeit his reward" (W. J. Conybeare) "but he himself shall escape as though he were pulled out of the fire" (Olaf M. Norlie on 1 Cor. 3:15). "For we must all appear before the judgment seat of Christ; that *every* one may receive the things done in his body, according to that he hath done, whether it be good or bad" (2 Cor. 5:10). Second Corinthians 4:17 determines that the troubles and sufferings of ours, in following the life of Christ, are quite small and won't last long but "bring with it a reward multiplied every way, loading us with everlasting glory" (Ronald Knox). With this in mind, we hear the words of God admonishing the believer, "The Lord recompense thy work, and a full reward will be given thee" (Ruth 2:12) and "look to yourselves, . . . that we may receive a full reward" (2 John 8). *A full reward!* Have you ever thought deeply about what God and Paul meant when in Philippians 3:13-14 we hear of "the prize" that was the one thing to which Paul devoted his entire life and every effort? After Paul's conversion he was determined to lay all aside—leave everything behind to make certain he received, "the prize." (It is significant that most scholars translate it "the prize of the *upward, heavenly,* or *heavenward* call or summons," author's italics.) Those receiving this "prize" will do so in heaven. What is "the prize" that is worth every believer's absolute, fullest stretch while here upon this earth?

Is it SALVATION? Obviously Philippians 3:14 and 1 Corinthians 9:24 are written to people already saved.

Is it HEAVEN? It cannot be heaven because heaven is obtained only by grace, not by works.

Is it RESURRECTION? No, because every saved, heaven-bound person is already promised the resurrection.

Is it REWARDS? The emphasis and focus are upon a single reward/prize, not all the different types of rewards.

Is not the summum bonum, "the prize," of earthly life's works the full reward?

This view is totally consistent with the teachings and life of Paul. Also, this conviction is in complete harmony with the teachings of Jesus about the number-one *(protos)* place in heaven (Matt. 20:25-28). "The prize" of the "upward calling" to be "the full reward" in no wise contradicts the teachings of our Lord or the Bible.

Since there is a *full* reward in heaven, then there must *then* be also less than a full reward in heaven. This point is strengthened by the fact that it is entirely possible that we believers can suffer "loss" in eternity, even though we are saved and headed for eternal inheritances and blessings. Is it not thoroughly logical and biblical that less than a full reward in eternity is caused by this "loss" that a believer may sustain? And isn't such a "loss" due to the believer's failure to live according to the pattern of the Christ life? I say yes.

The point at which we run the risk of eternal loss seems *not* to be in the realm of what I have called "general" inheritance and blessings but loss in the realm of that something more—the "full reward." Therefore, even though all believers are equal in many ways in their eternal inheritance, all believers are not equal in all ways.

As Jesus speaks in Matthew 5:19 it is obvious that He is speaking of life here on earth in relationship to life hereafter in the kingdom of Heaven. Our Lord is clear to express the fact that there will be "the least in the kingdom of heaven" and "great in the kingdom of heaven." James Moffatt translates it as "*ranked great in the Realm of heaven*" (author's italics). Also Matthew 18:4 adds to this distinction, "Whosoever therefore shall humble himself as this little child, the same is greatest in the kingdom of heaven." Adding to this, the Bible speaks of the judgment of the believer's earthly works in 2 Corinthians 5:10. Why must all believers appear before Christ to have works tested and judged if all believers are equal, the same, and nothing done here makes for a difference there? Apparently there is a difference. The Bible further amplifies the difference in 1 Corinthians 3:13-14 as it speaks of "rewards" compared to "loss." Jesus Himself emphasizes the lack of equality in heaven in Matthew 20:26-27, as He compares "great" and "chief" among those in heaven. (The original text is even more revealing at this point where it uses *protos*, meaning number one instead of chief.) God has a desire for every believer to be one of those greats throughout all eternity and has made all factors available here on earth to make us so! You may have heard someone say, "I'll just be happy to get into heaven by the skin of my teeth!" But is that not a sacrilegious way to look at God's great plan and God's great price in Jesus?

Two Important Questions

#1: Think about Jesus' story concerning the workers in the vineyard in Matthew 20:1-16. Doesn't this say there is equality for all in heaven, regardless? No, absolutely not. This account is sandwiched between two verses which make the same point—"the last shall be first and the first last" (20:16, also see 19:30). Therefore, the vineyard workers are illustrative to stress the possibility of last first and first last, but not equality for all in heaven. The lessons to be learned from the Matthew 20 passage are:

(a) There are rewards.
(b) The rewards are based upon our works (after salvation) here.
(c) Rewards are based upon God's standards, not man's.
(d) The Lord rewards "whatsoever is right" (vv. 4,7).
(e) The first here has the possibility of being last there and vice versa. To use this text to stress equality for all in heaven is a misuse. Also a careful study of the often misunderstood passages of Matthew 24:51; 25:30; and Luke 12:46 will keep one from becoming confused and distracted concerning the servant life.

#2: Can it really be heaven if all are not equal? Will there not be envy, strife, jealously, covetousness, and division? Heaven will be a place of perfection where we are finally conformed to the image of Christ and therefore God will have eliminated all such character flaws as envy, strife, jealousy, covetousness, and division. Further, I believe, there will be so much of God's love in heaven that there will be no place for such earthly feelings. We may be assured that God's reward system is not for punishment but for praise!

The Full Eternal Inheritance

There may be some unclear areas as to last things but one thing is absolutely clear—there is a full reward in heaven and the Lord wants us to have it. But what is this "full reward" of our inheritance?

Jesus is presently at the right hand of the throne of God (Heb. 12:2; Acts 7:55-56). Christ says, "I . . . am set down with my Father in his throne" (Rev. 3:21). In speaking to the body of Christ, our Lord encourages us to be more than ordinary Christians cooled off by the compromise of the world (Rev. 3:14-20). Then Jesus seems surely to be pointing toward the full reward for those who overcome as He overcame when He declares, "To him that overcometh will I grant to sit with me in my throne, even as I also overcame, and am set down with my Father in his throne" (Rev. 3:21). In light of these words of our Lord and also the text that will follow, it seems certain that the full reward is both—all that comes with the "general" inheritance but also an additional special place of sitting with Christ as corulers and coreigners throughout eternity.

"We shall also reign with him" (2 Tim. 2:12). Our coreigning and coruling is further emphasized in Zechariah 3:7 and Revelation 20:4,6. (Even though many believe this reference is to the millennium it, nonetheless, emphasizes the fact of reigning.) Revelation 22:3-5 continues to underscore reigning with Christ.

The question might be asked, "Are not all believers going to reign and rule in heaven?" If all believers in heaven are involved in some sort of reigning and ruling, it is certain that those of "full reward" will have a particularly special place of reigning and ruling (Matt. 5:19; 18:4; 20:26-27). Does this grip us? Beloved, think of it, it is possible for the servant/intercessor to sit in a special place of coreigning and coruling with Christ!!

Over what exactly is it possible to coreign and corule? R. C. H. Lenski refers the full reward to the believer's payday or reward in heaven, saying, "It (the full reward) is the reward of grace which is mentioned in Luke 19:17 and 19. It will certainly be full to overflowing." Lenski confirms the relationship of coreigning and coruling to the full reward. Coreigning and coruling will be over "many things" (Matt. 25:21-23). It appears that rule and authority will be over the world and angels according to 1 Corinthians 6:1-4. Romans 8:17 declares that we are "joint-heirs with Christ" and in Christ all things are ours, "things present or things to come" (1 Cor. 3:21-23). We can see the possibility of us becoming coruler and coreigner over all as indicated in Luke 12:42-44. In Matthew 19:27-28 we see that the apostles shall corule and coreign from twelve thrones while Luke 19 speaks of the good and faithful servant that is given reign over as many as ten cities. *
Jesus makes it clear that there will be those to reign and rule with Him and to sit on His right hand and left hand as He clarifies the kingdom to the mother of James and John in Matthew 20:20-23.

How to Receive the Full Reward of Coruling

There is but one key and one secret to this special place of coruling and coreigning in the kingdom. Jesus makes this secret irrefutably plain in Matthew 20:25-28. The life on earth that leads to coreigning and coruling with Christ, in His kingdom of heaven throughout eternity, is the life of the servant! This is the servant life! We must clearly understand that the inherited privilege of coreigning and coruling with Christ is based upon a

*Realize that the "citizens" of verse 14 are the "enemies" of verse 27 and is a reference to the lost who are cut off and have, of course, no part in reigning and ruling.

faithful and trustworthy servant life here on earth (Matt. 25:21-23; Luke 12:42-44; 16:10-12; 19:11-19; 1 Cor. 6:2; 2 Thess. 1:4-5).

The following story illustrates the great truth of Luke 12:48 which says, "For unto whomsoever much is given, of him shall be much required."

This, of course, is much easier said than done. We, in the same way as James and John, fight against the old man within us.

For the Christian to live a servant life patterned after Jesus' life will take discipline, but the full reward will be worth a million times a million of our dedicated efforts!

Some years ago the newspapers reported a man had died in a Chicago hospital, a pauper patient. After his death it was discovered that his ragged clothes were filled with money. Bills were sewn under the patches, gold pieces lined the coat collar. When the investigation was finished, several thousand dollars had been brought to light. Who was responsible for his pauperism? The man himself! So shall it be with us as believers in the eternal kingdom, if we fail to live out the servant life here on earth so obviously defined through the Word of our Lord. Isn't it a wonderful thing to observe that Jesus did not scold or rebuke the mother of Zebedee's children but instead explained how one might receive the highest places of coreigning and coruling with Him in the kingdom!

In Summary:

- There is no equality in heaven because there will be "least" and "great" there.
- The servant life of Christ here on earth is the basis for greatness throughout eternity.
- The Christian servant who is good and faithful upon this earth will be rewarded with all the "general" blessings and inheritances but will also receive a particularly special place of coreigning and coruling with Christ in eternity.

• The "greats" will undoubtedly receive the "full reward."

Again, there may be some further discussion about eschatology, but one fact is absolutely clear—the fullest reward in heaven is based upon the servant life here on earth.

PART III
The Sacrificed Life Is a
DISCIPLINE

And Jesus said unto him, No man, having put his
hand to the plow, and looking back, is fit for the kingdom
of God.   *Luke 9:62*

11 | THE SERVANT'S PRICE

Ye are bought with a price; be ye not the servants of men (1 Cor. 7:23).

What? know ye not that your body is the temple of the Holy Ghost which is in you, which ye have of God, and ye are not your own? (1 Cor. 6:19).

The last time the tomb of George Washington at Mount Vernon was officially entered, before the body was removed to the present mausoleum, was on the occasion of General Lafayette's last visit to the United States in 1824. The General stood in the presence of the departed Washington, who had been his beloved comrade in the cause of liberty. Lafayette accidently cut his finger and noticed the blood on it, held it up, and exclaimed to the officers who were acting as his bodyguard, "Gentlemen, the price of liberty!"

Those who set out to discipline their lives while living the sacrificed life must never forget there is also a price to be paid for the servant of Christ. How is the servant of Christ related to a price? Matthew 20:26-28 refers to "the ransom" and that ransom speaks directly of the servant's price. Every day we ask, "How much is that and how much does it cost?" The child of God needs to look again and again at the price paid for himself. When we see the price paid for us it should make us rejoice and want to serve Him with all of our heart!

For ye are bought with a price: therefore glorify God in your body, and in your spirit, which are God's (1 Cor. 6:20).

Wherefore gird up the loins of your mind, be sober, and hope to the end for the grace that is to be brought unto you at the revelation of Jesus Christ; As obedient children, not fashioning yourselves according to the former lusts in your ignorance: But as he which hath called you is holy, so be ye holy in all manner of conversation; Because it is written, Be ye holy; for I am holy. And if ye call on the Father, who without respect of persons judgeth according to every man's work, pass the time of your sojourning here in fear: Forasmuch as ye know that ye were not redeemed with corruptible things, as silver and gold, from your vain conversation received by tradition from your fathers; But with the precious blood of Christ as of a lamb without blemish and without spot: Who verily was forordained before the foundation of the world, but was manifest in these last times for you (1 Pet. 1:13-20).

In these verses of Scripture we have the great appeal for the servant life. First Corinthians 6:19 says that we are not our own! How true that is. You did not will to live. Why are you not a leper lying on the side of some street in India? You had nothing to do with that. "You are not your own!" You do not sustain your life. One wrong kind of germ into your system and your life is over. "You are not your own!" Christian, you did not redeem yourself. No, it is not by anything we do, lest we would boast about it. "You are not your own!" Yes, the truth is that you are bought with a price and you are not your own.

Can you picture a slave on the slave market about to be bought for a price? This person could have become a slave for sale due to poverty where his parents may have sold him into slavery, because of a crime, and slavery was the sentence, or perhaps he had sold himself for some reason. Imagine, this slave had previously been owned by a cruel master. On the inside and outside of this slave's body are the scars of abuse and mishandling. (You know we were slaves once to a cruel master—to self, to sin, and to Satan.) Then the slave, as he stands on the auction block, sees in the crowd a buyer whom he has heard—a master who is kind, loving, and provides well for his own.

The slave on the auction block cries out with all that is within him, "If you will but pay the price for me I will go home with you, I will go anywhere for you, I will do anything." And at that moment the kind, loving master turns and says, "I'll pay the price for that one." And Jesus, lover of our souls, says, "I'll pay the price for that soul!" We are not our own, we are bought with a price. We all have a master. When people say, "I will do what I please," usually what they mean is that they cannot help but serve a habit or passion that has control over them. We are not to be looking for freedom from a master; we are looking for a good master whom we love and have freedom to serve! The Christian servant thinks not of his rights but of his debt.

When Jesus exclaimed from the cross "It is finished" (John 19:30), He was saying that the debt had been paid in full for His servants. We are not our own, we have been bought with a price; therefore, we should rejoice and want to serve our Master.

> I saw One hanging on a tree, In agony and blood; He fixed
>   His languid eyes on me, As near the cross I stood.
> Sure, never, till my latest breath, Can I forget that look:
> It seemed to charge me with His death, Tho' not a word He
>   spoke.
> My conscience felt and owned the guilt, And plunged me in
>   despair;
> I saw my sins His blood had split, And helped to nail Him
>   there.
> Alas I knew not what I did, but now my tears are vain,
> Where shall my trembling soul be hid, for I the Lord have
>   slain.
> A second look He gave, which said, "I freely all forgive;
> This blood is for thy ransom paid, I die that thou may'st live."
> Oh, can it be upon a tree, the Saviour paid the price for me?
> My soul is thrilled, my heart is filled, to think He died for me.
> Yes, you dear Saviour have paid the price for me.
> Now I freely choose to abide, as thy servant, forever to be.

There is a song, "Happy day, happy day, When Jesus washed my sins away!" It is a happy day when we realize the price paid and that we have such a privilege to be a servant of One who loved us enough to pay such a price for us as His own servant!

12 | THE SERVANT'S CALL

Let every man abide in the same calling wherein he was called. Art thou called being a servant? care not for it: but if thou mayest be made free, use it rather. For he that is called in the Lord, being a servant, is the Lord's freeman: likewise also he that is called, being free, is Christ's servant. Ye are bought with a price; be not ye the servants of men. Brethren, let every man, wherein he is called, therein abide with God (1 Cor. 7:20-24).

As surely as there is a claim upon us, because of the price paid by our Savior, there is a call upon us because our Savior's greatest desire is for us to abide as His servant. We will see how this claim is linked with His call upon us, and both will usher us into the servants' quarters and the discipline of that life.

You and I have been bought as bondslaves. Even though we have our freedom as sons and heirs, we are not to disobey the disciplined life but continue in the joy of the bondslave life.

There were several types of servants in biblical days. When God refers to our being a servant to Jesus and Himself, He uses a very special word, *doulos*, meaning bondslave. The bondservant that Christ is looking for is pictured in the Old Testament texts, Deuteronomy 15:12-16 and Exodus 21:1-6.

This "doulos" life-style is to be the burning desire and discipline of every believer.

1. Jesus is saying to become a doulos for this is where greatness lies with Him and in the kingdom to come (Matt. 20:27).
2. God said that His dear Son became a *doulos* in His earthly ministry (Phil. 2:5-11).

84

3. Paul is saying he was doing what Jesus did and what He told us to do (1 Cor. 9:19).
4. The Bible says to abide and continue serving the Lord as a doulos (1 Cor. 7:20-24).

So you see, servanthood *(doulos)* is *the place.* It is the place God and Christ desires *every* believer to live out his earthly existence. It is the place of great blessing—here and in eternity!

Let us recognize several don'ts at this point:

1. *Don't* get confused at Galatians 4:1-7. This passage does not negate the *doulos* life-style believer, even though we are sons and heirs. This passage is the picture of an immature Christian who appears to still be a bondslave to the old life. Verse 6 is saying this should not be; we should be bondslaves to the new way of life.
2. *Don't* draw back or recoil from the call to the *doulos* life. Some may say, "I'm afraid that I'll lose my job or my family will be changed or I will be broken or I'll have to take a vow of poverty or I'll look like a fool or it will cost me all." In truth, there is no guarantee that this will not happen but it does not always happen that way. Besides, look at the price paid and hear the call made. Yes, whatever it costs, the *doulos* life is the place of obedience, peace, joy, and blessing! The reason the idea of the slave is repulsive to some of us is because we remember, all too well, how we were treated by our old master of sin, self, and Satan. He was a cruel master. He promised pleasure but it was only for a season. We found the way of the transgressor to be hard and we found the wages of such a life is death and separation from true life. Satan lied about the servant life, like he lies about everything else, in order to try to murder us and our happiness (John 6:44). The bondslave is the position of a son and heir. No wonder we have joy in being His bondslave! No wonder we are willing to serve Him even though we have freedom as a son and heir! In the Bible days the bondslave was trustworthy, obedient, and one in whom the master had confidence. He was given much freedom and responsibility. Bondslaves were often made guardians, custodians, managers, stewards, and governors over all the affairs of the master. (This is the pic-

ture in Galatians 4:1-7.) Someone might say, "Oh well, if that's the case and I'm going to be in charge, then I'm willing to be a bondslave." But you must remember this type of privileged status only came to those who were humble, obedient, and faithful.

3. *Don't* think that as sons and heirs we are free from responsibility. We are not free *from* responsibility—we are free *in* the responsibility as bondslaves who have the standing of being sons and heirs. It could not be any better. That is why we abide as *doulos!*

How do we get to the place of abiding as a *doulos?* Jesus gives us the key in Matthew 6:24 where He says we cannot serve two masters. We must choose. Joshua earlier made this very point in Joshua 24:15 when he said, "Choose you this day whom ye will serve." We must choose to abide as a bondslave.

Next, we must make ourselves a *doulos*. Philippians 2:7 says that Jesus made Himself a servant. First Corinthians 9:19 says Paul made himself a servant, indicating they had to choose and make themselves servants. The *doulos* life is a deliberate, willful, abiding life as His bondslave. Another thing to remember is the Greek word *eutheos* (Mark 1:18). This is a servant's word meaning *forthwith, straightway, immediately*. This is the way the servant obeys and abides. *Straightway* and *immediately* they put aside their nets and followed Him. Often there is a great loss between the call and the coming. This is not so with the abiding bondslave. He immediately chooses to abide as *doulos* at the feet of Christ.

See how beautifully and clearly this willful act of abiding as *doulos* is portrayed in the passages of Deuteronomy 15:12-16 as well as in Exodus 21:1-6. You can see in these passages that once a servant made the willful choice to abide there was an impressive ceremony, a permanent scar, a badge of honor, and a testimony of undying love. Jesus saw this *doulos* role for His earth life. He was free on earth as a Son and Heir. He chose (in spite of His freedom) to abide as *doulos* before the Father. There was an impressive ceremony, horrible and cruel as it may have been. He personally and plainly said with His life, "I love the Father." There was a public scarring when He went willingly to the doorpost called Calvary. The scars of Christ's *doulos* life remain to this day. We shall know Him by the nailprints in His hands!

Now why did Christ, the Son of God, abide as a *doulos?* Exodus 21:5 has the answer. It was love, the same as the bondslave in Deuteronomy and Exodus. Love for His master—the Father. Love for His wife/bride—the church. Love for the children—His offspring. Out of the motivation of love, in the midst of all of His freedom as Son and Heir, Christ willfully chose to abide as a bondslave to His Master's will. Jesus calls the believer today to that same doulos life, "as the Father has sent me, so send I you."

Now see how clearly the Christian life and Jesus' life parallel these two Old Testament passages. At salvation we are made sons and heirs. We continued to be free to choose to abide in Him or stray from Him. If we choose to abide there will be an impressive ceremony. Perhaps no human may attend, but you can be assured that all of heaven will be in attendance on the day we willfully choose to forever abide as the *doulos* for Christ. We will personally and plainly say, "I love my Master, His bride the church, and His children more than anything else." And we will be willing to have the public markings of a bondslave. We are not ashamed of a public display at the doorpost. We remember that it was at the doorpost in the land of Egypt that the blood was sprinkled. That was the doorpost of blood, commitment, obedience, self-denial, and suffering. Praise God, it was the doorpost of life! And we remember Calvary as the doorpost where the blood was sprinkled. It, too, was the doorpost of blood, of self-denial, of sacrifice, of suffering, of obedience, and of life! Jesus says that His disciples are marked, for His sheep know His voice and they hear Him and they follow Him. The *doulos* life is a badge of honor, a testimony of undying love, and the life of joy and blessing!

Harry Ironside drew a vivid mental picture of a bondslave couple and their servants' quarters that is linked with these two Old Testament passages.

> Imagine with me the sunset years of a happy couple we shall call the servant John and the wife Mary. The family has grown up. In the evening John returns from the fields into their love-filled home in the valley. The sun has just sunk behind the hills and the long shadows are darkening the room where Mary sits looking for the return of John. She has placed his favorite chair before the fireplace with its cheery flickering flame. As John returns and settles down in his chair, Mary quietly slips up behind him, and gently strokes his forehead, and runs her fingers lovingly through his graying hair. Her hands slip over his ears, and her fingers once more fondle the precious scars made by the awl so many years ago. The tears begin to fall, for she recalls the meaning of those scars, and she whispers in his pierced ear, 'Oh John, I love you more than I ever thought I could.' And then she stoops to plant a . . . , but wait, some scenes are too holy, too sacred for others to behold, so we turn away and leave the loving couple dreaming in the glow of the happy days.

And it will be a thousand times more tender and holy and sacred than this scene—when the willful, abiding bondslave of Christ steps just inside the gates of glory and feels the Master's nail-scarred, *doulos* hands as He touches the place of our life that marked the day we chose forever to abide as His *doulos* and then hear Him whisper, "Well done, thou good and faithful bondslave, enter thou into the joy of thy Lord."

> I love, I love my Master,
> I will not go out free,
> For He is my Redeemer;
> He paid the price for
> me . . .
> My Master shed His
> life-blood
> My servant life to win

And save me from the
  bondage
  Of tyrant self and sin.
He chose me for His service,
  And gave me power to
  choose
That blessed, perfect
  freedom,
  Which I shall never
  lose . . .
I love, I love my Master,
  I will not go out free!
        —Author unknown

13 | THE SERVANT'S KING

And the king's servants said unto the king, Behold, they servants are ready to do whatsoever my lord the king shall appoint (2 Sam. 15:15).

But it shall not be so among you: but whosoever will be great among you, let him be your minister (Matt. 20:26).

We are now ready to consider life in the servants' quarters. Have you ever lived in servants' quarters? Have you ever looked into servants' quarters? Do you think you might enjoy life in the servants' quarters? When we hear what Jesus says in Matthew 20:26 we begin to realize that life in the servants' quarters is to be our new home as a believer. And when we begin to live in the servants' quarters that means leaving behind some old things and taking up some new things. How can I possibly do such a thing? (Remember now we are not talking about being saved, we are talking about saved people who are living a disciplined servant's life.) Say these words, "Behold, thy servants are ready to do whatsoever my lord the king shall appoint." What a great and marvelous thing if all Christians would say this and mean it. I believe it was Francis Dixon who said such a text as this reflects the personal relationship of "the King's servant."

David is a type of our King. David's servants recognized the fact that they did have a king and a master over them. David's servants were 600 foreign soldiers who loved him and were loyal to him as their new master. They were saying, "You are our king and we love you and we'll be loyal to you." That is exactly what the believer is to be saying day by day to King Jesus. We were once foreigners, outsiders, outcasts, rebels, but Jesus is our new King. He is our Master and we are servants. We love Him and will be loyal to Him. This seems to be the way Paul felt in 1 Corinthians 15:9-10. On the one hand he recognized he was an unfit foreigner, outcast, outsider, and rebel but he had become a servant to a new King and Master and it was, "But by the grace of God I am what I am: and his grace which was bestowed upon me was not in vain; but I laboured more abundantly than they all: yet not I, but the grace of God which was with me" (v. 10). He was saying, "I love You and I'm going to be Your loyal servant!"

Also 2 Samuel 15:15 says those who totally surrender "are ready." Surrender, full and absolute and unreserved. This is the thrust of Romans 6:13,16-22. Servants are to surrender all and to be ready.

> Ready to go, ready to stay,
>   Ready my place to fill;
> Ready for service, lowly or great,
>   Ready to do His will.
>
> Ready to suffer grief or pain,
>   Ready to stand the test;
> Ready to stay at home and send
>   Others, if he sees best.
>
> Ready to go, ready to bear,
>   Ready to watch and pray;
> Ready to stand aside and give,
>   Till he shall clear the way.
>
> Ready to speak, ready to think,
>   Ready with heart and brain;
> Ready to stand where he sees fit,
>   Ready to stand the strain.
>
> Ready to speak, ready to warn,
>   Ready o'er souls to yearn;
> Ready in life, ready in death,
>   Ready for his return.
>
> —A. C. Palmer

Someone asked William Booth to what did he attribute his spiritual success. He said, "There came a day when God got all."

"Finally, my brethren, be strong in the Lord, and in the power of his might (Eph. 6:10).

There is the story about a dwarf named Charlie Steinmetz who worked for Henry Ford. What Steinmetz lacked physically he made up in his electronic genius, and he built the huge electric generators that ran Henry Ford's first automobile factory. One day the large plant shut down and it was obviously an electrical problem. Ford used everyone he had on his staff to remedy the problem but no one was able. Finally, Steinmetz was recalled to the factory. He arrived, spent a few minutes fiddling and fooling around with a few electrical gadgets. The huge generators fired back up and the plant resumed operations. Steinmetz left. A few days later Henry Ford received a bill for $10,000. He thought that Steinmetz had charged him a bit too much so Ford sent a letter to that effect; explaining that Steinmetz was at the plant only a short time and just tinkered with a few wires which did not seem to be worth such a high cost. Soon Ford received Steinmetz's reply: "Dear Henry, for spending a few minutes and fooling with a few wires I charged you only $10. For knowing where to fool around and which wires to fool around with, I charged you $9,990."

Thinking and fooling around in the flesh are absolutely worthless. But knowing where the power lies and how to tap into that source is worth everything!

"Finally" is a Greek imperative—a command to obey—an absolute urgent and necessary obedience. Paul stands now as a seasoned soldier communicating urgent, necessary orders from the Commander of all of us.

"Be strong in the Lord, and in the power of his might" (Eph. 6:10). God has special aspects of Himself for great spiritual conflicts we may encounter. He is able! First John 5:20, "We are in him that is true," we are in Him Who is able. That is exactly why we can claim Luke 18:1, "That men ought always to pray and not to faint." First John 4:4 says, "Greater is he that is in you, than he that is in the world." Colossians 1:11 says, "Strength-ened with all might, according to his glorious power."

After reading Ephesians 1:15-23, every believer should be able to get a glimpse of the power of Christ that dwells in him!

You may be saying, "But I feel so weak and helpless." Well then read 2 Timothy 1:7-8. It is the power of God on which we will rely, not upon ourselves. Second Timothy 2:1 tells us that God's strength is a "grace" gift, unmerited power.

Someone else may say, "But it's so rough and tough in the place where I have to live and work!" Then read Romans 5:20, "Where sin abounded, grace did much more abound." The tougher the place the more the grace gift of unmerited power!

"But I have so little strength." Then read Revelation 3:8 and see what God did with those having "a little strength." That little strength pleased Him. It shut doors; it opened doors. He blessed the "little." He blesses it, He uses it. It's amazing what God can do with our "little" when He applies His grace gift of unmerited power to it and we do as those in Revelation 3:8, "hast kept my word, and hast not denied my name."

How is it that we get the "little" strength? It is through those essential elements of intimacy (aloneness, obedience, and the Word). Read 2 Corinthians 12:9-10 and 2 Corinthians 10:4, we are mighty through God to the pulling down of strongholds! Careful now, don't become one of those "cocky Christians" who feels there is no way he can fail. We must always remember what 1 Corinthians 10:12 says just as well as verse 13.

"Man, I've got it together now!" You do? Wonderful! But don't ever forget this place of power, at the feet of Jesus. Spiritual strength is based upon our union with Christ. Remember that Ephesians 6:10 says, "Finally, my brethren, be strong in the Lord." This place of power and strength is for the saved who are living the Christ life. What a union! All spiritual strength is based upon this union in Christ. John 14:20, "I am in my Father, and ye in me." And that is exactly the union spoken of in John 15:4-7. We must remember that we are the servants of the King, and apart from the King we can do nothing (John 15:5).

14 | THE SERVANT'S VIEW

And he turned him unto his disciples, and said privately, Blessed
are the eyes which see the things that ye see (Luke 10:23).

While we look not at the things which are seen, but at the things
which are not seen: for the things which are seen are temporal;
but the things which are not seen are eternal (2 Cor. 4:18).

For the invisible things of him from the creation of the world are
clearly seen, being understood by the things that are made,
even his eternal power and Godhead; so that they are without
excuse (Rom. 1:20).

And Elisha prayed, and said, Lord, I pray thee, open his eyes,
that he may see. And the Lord opened the eyes of the young
man; and he saw: and, behold, the mountain was full of horses
and chariots of fire round about Elisha (2 Kings 6:17).

Now faith is the substance of things hoped for, the evidence of
things not seen (Heb. 11:1).

The Bible makes it clear that some have seen the unseen.
Balaam's donkey saw an angel of the Lord and later Balaam
himself saw the angel of the Lord (Num. 22:21-23). Elisha saw
the supernatural departure of Elijah (2 Kings 2:10-11). Elisha
saw the Lord's hosts at Dothan (2 Kings 6:15-16). The servant of
Elisha also saw this supernatural hosts of chariots of fire. Isaiah
saw the Lord upon His throne and angels (Isa. 6:1). Abraham
saw the day of the Lord. That was through faith, type, and a
special view (see John 8:56.) Paul was interested in seeing the
unseen (2 Cor. 4:18). Moses saw Jesus as One who is invisible

(Heb. 11:27). The Book of Revelation is a description of John seeing the whole future of the world. Yes, some have seen the unseen!

The view as a bondslave from the servants' quarters has to do with eyesight—spiritual eyesight. There are two ways to view life. One is that we may see only that which is visible to the physical eye. If this is our view of the world we are doomed to a slow process of degeneration and rot. But, praise God, there is another way! The other way to view life is to see the invisible. To see the invisible is the key to eternal life, to overcoming, to enduring, and it is the only way to view life as the bondslave. In fact Hebrews 11:1 tells us that faith is the conviction and confidence of the unseen. Jesus said that He was "grieved for the hardness of their hearts" (Mark 3:5). The servant's view is when unseen spiritual eyes are fixed upon unseen spiritual things (2 Cor. 4:18).

Before spiritual eyesight becomes a reality, the lost man must "see" himself in need of a Savior and be saved. Afterwards, the saved man must "see" himself hungering and thirsting for an intimate walk with his Lord!

Who Sees the Unseen?

Are we all to see such unseen things as described in the Bible? Ephesians 1:18 and 2 Corinthians 5:7 lead us to believe that faith does have illuminating power. I remember very well the first-hand account of a national evangelist, Abel Mwakikomili, in the midst of a great revival in Africa recently. While pushing his motorbike across a small foot bridge he slipped and began to fall. He was helplessly gripping the bridge with one hand and holding onto his treasured motorbike with the other, hanging in great peril. At that moment, although he had encountered no other travelers, a woman appeared behind him. Even though this African preacher could not speak the language of that particular remote area the woman spoke his own tribal language. She reassured him, reached down, and with unusual strength aided him and his motorbike to safety. When he looked around, the woman was gone. The preacher declared that this was an angel of the Lord! Regardless of the origin, this man was seeing with spiritual eyes.

Just this week I heard a former persecuted and tortured prisoner from Romania give his testimony of being locked in a pitch-black dungeon cell and then assaulted by many flesh-eating rats. In the darkness he cried out to God for help. He declared that at that moment the room was filled with light, and an angel of the Lord assured him that he had no reason to fear; then the room was dark again. The rats were nowhere to be felt from that moment on. Later, the jailer came to the room, turned on the lights, and, to both the jailer and the prisoner's astonishment, all the rats were dead and in one pile in the room.

A believer released from a Lithuanian prison where he had been sentenced for his faith, wrote; "My outward appearance is not attractive. In the slave labor camp I worked beneath the earth and had an accident which broke my back. I later went to visit a Christian family. One of the children stared at me and asked, 'Uncle, what do you have on your back?' Sure that some mockery would follow, I answered, 'A hunch back.' 'No,' said the child, 'God is love and gives no one deformities. You do not have a hunch back, but a box below your shoulders. In this box are angelic wings. Someday the box will open and you will fly to heaven with these wings.' I began to cry for joy. Even now as I write I am crying."

Did this child not see God with spiritual eyes? I think so! Do you see more than just with human eyes? Do you see Christ and God at work? Do you have unseen eyes that are fixed upon unseen things? "We need to pray that things that are seen shall become transparent so that through them we shall see the things eternal" (Amy Carmichael). This was the prayer of Elisha in 2 Kings 6:17, "Lord, I pray thee, open his eyes, that he may see." Sometime ago I began to pray for spiritual eyesight in a fourfold way. "Lord please make my eyes spiritual enough so as to see: every man as only a soul—nothing more and nothing less; every material thing as only manure—nothing more and nothing less; to be able to see the warfare of the spiritual world; and see myself as a broken bondslave of Christ—nothing more and nothing less."

It has been said that our trials and troubles and temptations often seem so terrible because our spiritual vision is so limited. We must agree with that. If we had keen enough spiritual vision we would never again even speak of sacrifice and self-denial.

What Is to Be Seen?

But what unseen things should spiritual eyes of the bondslave see?

The Earth

When the bondslave rises from his bed and peers out the window or opens the door and gazes into a new day, he should see the earth as preparation for all eternity. To the believer this earth is but a training place for eternity. We must see clearly this great truth, for it affects every area of our lives as Christians. Colossians 3:22-25 expresses this importance. The beautiful quarry illustration from 1 Kings 6:7 is appropriate. Nothing could illustrate our purpose for earthly existence better than this passage in which the reference is made to Solomon's temple. At a considerable distance from the actual building site of the temple the stonecutters shaped the stones according to the designer's plan. Undoubtedly in the quarry there were the inescapable noises of breaking, blasting, dragging, rolling, tumbling, chipping, sawing, cutting, chiseling, cracking, washing, and cleansing. All of this was absolutely necessary for the stones' shining, polished uniqueness and admirable ornateness in order to be well fitted for the temple. However, when those beautiful stones came together at the temple there was no need for the noise of the quarry. The quarry work had already been accomplished in order that the future temple might have every stone rightly fitted.

Is not the earth the place where God does His quarry work preparing us for our place in eternity? Yes, I believe so. Therefore, you should think of yourselves as living stones (1 Pet. 2:5).

What a joy to "see" that a believer is created for God's loving, lasting purpose. This is the same light in which S. D. Gordon saw it. The bondslave sees life now as an apprenticeship for service throughout eternity. He is trained now to be a tested, trusted, trained coruler with Christ in eternity. The believer on earth is in a college getting ready for the great commencement day. Yes dear friend, this life is technical training for throne reigning. (And it is true that this may explain why some of the best and most godly die young—they have completed their apprenticeship. School is out here on earth, and they have been promoted on up to eternity.)

Self

Self is another thing that the bondslave must see with spiritual eyes. What a joy to see ourselves with spiritual eyes. To do so is to be relieved from man-made expectations and burdens, to be secure in the Lord and filled with peacefulness that only the *doulos* of Christ can ever know!

We are "called to be saints [set apart]" (1 Cor. 1:2). And the Bible further says that we are set apart as "a peculiar people" (1 Pet. 2:9). Isaiah 49:5 speaks, in part, to why these peculiar people are set apart, "the Lord that formed me from the womb to be his servant." We are sons and heirs with all the attendant freedoms, but we have chosen to use that freedom to carry out our role and our responsibility through the bondslave life just like our dear Master. The following is a beautiful passage used to give insight into how we should view ourselves as bondslaves with spiritual eyes. "But which of you, having a servant plowing or feeding cattle, will say unto him by and by, when he is come from the field, Go and sit down to meat? And will not rather say unto him, Make ready wherewith I may sup, and gird thyself, and serve me, till I have eaten and drunken; and afterward thou shalt eat and drink? Doth he thank that servant because he did the things that were commanded him? I trow not. So likewise ye, when ye shall have done all those things which are commanded you, say, We are unprofitable servants: we have done that which was our duty to do" (Luke 17:7-10).

Brokenness

Verse 7 indicates that this bondslave has already been broken. To be broken does not seem, on the surface, to be such a wonderful thing. But have you ever known the joy of being broken, washed, released, lifted, blessed, and anointed? If you have, then you understand the unspeakable blessing of brokenness. We will talk more about brokenness when we later consider humility. Many things are piled on the bondslave in verses 7-8. The bondslave is to expect such. As soon as the *doulos* begins to murmur, complain, and grumble he ceases to be a pleasing servant of his master. We may groan but we cannot complain. The joy is that there will be no more placed upon us than we are able to bear (1 Cor. 10:13). What exceeding joy! Our Master already knows our load limit.

Thanklessness

No thanks is the immediate reward as indicated in verse 9. Must we always have our thanks here and now in the presence of other mere mortals? Are we not then seeking to please men? Remember it is the "hireling" that demands compensation on the spot and runs when the going gets rough. Not so with the *doulos*. He has had freedom to go the way of the world, but he has deliberately and willfully chosen not to run but to remain. Paul understood this very well as he declared, "I am a debtor" (Rom. 1:14). He acknowledged that since he was owing he should be the one giving thanks, not receiving them. And he so felt the burden of that debt that he was ready to go to Rome to do whatever it took to make Christ known (v. 15).

Receive joy from what Jesus told the laborers in the vineyard in Matthew 20:7, "Whatsoever is right, that you shall receive." God is debtor to no man. He will settle all His accounts rightly. Therefore we have no need to worry over things from man. At the end the Lord of the harvest said unto the servant, "Well done, thou good and faithful servant: thou hast been faithful over a few things, I will make thee ruler over many things: enter thou into the joy of thy Lord" (Matt. 25:21).

Selflessness

This has to do with selfishness as seen in Luke 17:10—"done all those things." This seems to be the picture of the bondslave who is all alone doing everything himself. It is so easy to feel as if no one else understands the servant role and is willing to help (this was Martha's problem). But do not condemn others when they fail to understand the servant life or seem to be selfish. Remember what Jesus said in Matthew 20:15, that the master could do what he would with his own. *The doulos life is personal, private, and individual.* What others do with the servant life is not your primary concern. *It is a question of what you will do.* When others fail to serve as bondslaves this only gives us more opportunities to serve Him and, consequently, the opportunity of becoming more like Christ who served all. "Finally, be ye all of one mind, having compassion one of another, love as brethren, be pitiful, be courteous: Not rendering evil for evil, or railing for railing: but contrariwise blessing; knowing that ye are thereunto called, that ye should inherit a blessing" (1 Pet. 3:8-9).

Unprofitable

Also Luke 17:10 speaks of the bondslave as being unprofitable. "I know that in me dwelleth no good thing" (Rom. 7:18). "What then? are we better than they? No, in nowise: for we have before proved both Jews and Gentiles, that they are all under sin; As it is written, There is none righteous, no, not one: There is none that understandeth, there is none that seeketh after God. They are all gone out of the way, they are together become unprofitable: there is none that doeth good, no, not one" (Rom. 3:9-12). There is nothing in us or about us that should cause boasting or independence. We are altogether unprofitable with one exception—the grace of God! What good we do have in us is due to the grace of God (1 Cor. 15:10).

Duty

Finally, the last part of Luke 17:10 speaks of "duty." The Master has every right to expect us to enact Romans 12:1 and present our bodies as a living sacrifice which is our reasonable and logical service or duty. "Friend, I do thee no wrong: didst not thou agree [on this]?" (Matt. 20:13).

> For though I preach the gospel, I have nothing to glory of: for necessity is laid upon me; yea, woe is unto me, if I preach not the gospel! For if I do this thing willingly, I have a reward: but if against my will, a dispensation of the gospel is committed unto me. What is my reward then? Verily that, when I preach the gospel, I may make the gospel of Christ without charge, that I abuse not my power in the gospel (1 Cor. 9:16-18).

Christ

> And he laid his hands on her: and immediately she was made straight, and glorified God (Luke 13:13).

The servant sees Jesus Christ as the Person who has mastered the servant. The very idea of servant declares the existence of a master. Jesus is to be our Savior *and* our Master! But mark this carefully, there is a great deal of difference between "master" and "mastered."

This can easily be seen in the life of the prodigal son's brother. The elder brother was under the roof of his father but not under the rule of his father. You see, he had a master but he was not mastered. A child may have a parent, but if that child is rebellious and disobedient, that child is not mastered by the parent. A horse may have a master because he has been bought on the auction block for a price, but the wild nature of that horse may be unbroken and he may continue being unmastered.

"Mastered" means to be ruled over and controlled—for someone to have authority and power over us. For the Christian, it means to be at the feet of Jesus ready to obey.

"And this I speak for your own profit; not that I may cast a snare upon you, but for that which is comely, and that ye may attend upon the Lord without distraction" (1 Cor. 7:35). "Anyone who lets himself be distracted from the work I plan for him is not fit for the Kingdom of God" (Luke 9:62, TLB). These texts are a clear picture of what it means to be a ready servant and not be distracted. There is a plain biblical illustration of both, how this should work and how it should not work. Martha was distracted while Mary had *chosen* to be undistracted and a ready servant (Luke 10:38-42). When I became gripped by this passage of Scripture I wrote to the Lord that I might be reminded.

> Lord, may I not be as dear Martha so "cumbered" with serving that I am dragged in so many different directions that I am distracted from the best, which is to attend You, without distraction. May I be always found conveniently at Your feet and by Your side.

> For what good use is a bondslave servant if he is not waiting and ready to serve immediately upon his master's call? Such a servant is not broken and mastered if he must be chased after, found, and begged to obey!

> But my sole desire is to "choose" as Mary "the good part which shall not be taken away." Oh, dear Lord, may the nearness to Your feet never be taken away from me.

I have the idea that many Christians are waiting for God to force them or whip them into becoming obedient bondslaves. That will never happen! What a wonderful Master we have the privilege of serving. He does not use such tactics to force obedience. We have a choice. We must choose ("plainly say, . . . I will not go out free"—Ex. 21:56. We choose to be saved. So then, we must choose to be obedient bondslaves.

Question: Doesn't our Master sometimes use force or take us to the proverbial "woodshed"? Yes, but that seems always to be for correction and for discipline. If the Lord must make us obey, then we cease to be willing servants because our free will has been violated. So the servant's view of Christ is, "Christ is the Master by whom I *choose* to be mastered!"

I was sitting alone in India with Rajamuthu, a man who had been raised by one of God's great *doulos* servants, Amy Carmichael. We were talking about the servant life. Pearl (as Amy had named him) said to me, drawing upon his remembrance of her, "If you earnestly continue to follow the servant life, then you will become unfamiliar." He meant the servant life requires the servant to decrease that Jesus might increase. Are we willing to become unfamiliar? Are we willing to be hidden? Are we willing to be missing? Are we willing to decrease? To be sure, this is not what the natural man will want to do.

Remember, it is impossible to do the unnatural without supernatural workings. It's like the coat and the mile and the cheek. It is impossible to be willing to give your coat and your cloak, to go one mile and then two miles, and to allow both cheeks to be slapped unless we have supernatural workings within us! Know this—such a life is not some unattainable ideal, but it is a practical life-style of one who has been mastered as *doulos*. Jesus is the only One who can live the Sermon on the Mount, and the only way you can live it is by being mastered by Him. This explains why often we are faced with impossible situations and called upon to do impossible things. (God is attempting to reduce us for Himself.) We are to give up and confess; we are to plainly say, "I will be mastered and not go free!"

Some might say, "I am not willing to lose coat or cloak, to go even one mile, or to have my cheeks slapped." Then there is but one reply to such a person. You are not mastered! Therefore, the work of God is being hindered, you are failing Christ right now, moment by moment, day by day, month by month, you are losing position to coreign and corule in eternity. But the unspeakable joy is that the Master waits to empower you with supernatural workings if you will plainly say, "I do not want to go free but only want to be mastered by Thee!"

15 | WILL

In everything give thanks: for this is the will of God in Christ Jesus concerning you (1 Thess. 5:18).

I am not interested in a life of show or only spiritual speech. Rather, I am interested in one that experiences the truth of God's Word, day by day and circumstance by circumstance. How does the bondslave view all the varied circumstances that confront him in life?

Let me again remind us of the quarry example in 1 Kings 6:7. During the entire seven years of the building of Solomon's temple in the holy city of Jerusalem "there was neither hammer nor ax nor any tool of iron heard in the house, while it was in building." We might ask, "How could this be?" The Bible says, "It was . . . made ready before it was brought thither."

That is, all the stones were cut and prepared on-site at the quarry in another place called Alexandria. The toiling, rough, painstaking labor was done in one place. When they were finally brought to the permanent site all the stones were perfectly fitted together in ease and peace, according to a master plan. We might say that the final finished product was the result of prefabrication preparations at another location. This is an apropos Old Testament illustration of the New Testament truth that God is now, while we are upon this earth, preparing us for corulership in eternity.

There are requirements emanating from quarry life. The stones require precise planning, careful handling, ornate designing, and often unique finishing. All these matters are appealing. Do we want to be stones like that in God's hands? Would we like to be such precious, well-finished stones for all eternity? I believe the answer is yes. But we must remember that these same stones cannot be allowed to escape certain other requirements of quarry life. *All* of this processing is absolutely necessary. I am certain we all understand which requirements usually must occur first.

According to 1 Thessalonians 5:16-19 we see what our response is to be in all circumstances. In verse 16 we are to "rejoice"; verse 17, we are to "pray"; verse 18, we are to "give thanks"; and verse 19, we are "to quench not the Spirit." These responses are to be forthcoming in the midst of whatever ensues. But how can a Christian truthfully respond in this way?

The question is this, "How can we handle or how shall we view the circumstances of life?" I think it boils down to the fact that the bondslave *accepts* all of life's circumstances as "quarry work." Paul saw this in Philippians 4:11-13, "Not that I speak in respect of want: for I have learned, in whatsoever state I am, therewith to be content. I know both how to be abased, and I know how to abound: everywhere and in all things I am instructed both to be full and to be hungry, both to abound and to suffer need. I can do all things through Christ which strengtheneth me." The Bible also teaches this in Romans 8:28. In our focal text, 1 Thessalonians 5:18, it is clarified for us. The only truthful way I know to live honestly by the teaching of such texts as these is to view all of life's circumstances as the *allowed will* of God. God has *allowed* these circumstances in our lives.

For me, the struggle to determine the "perfect" will of God and to distinguish that from the so-called "permissive" will of God— while at the same time desperately trying to understand all the inexplicable circumstances that happen—has all been absorbed into the undeniable and inescapable truth . . . God has *allowed all these things to happen!* I then am prepared to receive any and all things as being allowed to come into my life as quarry work. I just received a phone call that had *every* indication trouble was on the other end of the line. I said, "Lord, I receive this call, and I

rejoice in this call as You allowing it in my life for quarry work." I
believe that Job saw this, Paul saw it, Jesus saw it, too, and
many, many others are seeing it. This view of God's will is essential for the bondslave life.

Someone might ask, "Isn't this a passive and cowering spiritual posture?" No, it is not. It is thoroughly consistent and in harmony with the preaching of Jesus. Christ taught that if we're
demanded our coat, we're also to give our cloak. If we're compelled to go one mile we are to help me go two. If we are struck
on the right cheek we are to turn the left cheek. To accept this as
the allowed will of God does not mean that I do not feel the cold
when I am without my coat and cloak and that I do not feel the
sting, having been hit on both cheeks, or the drudgery of trudg-
ing on two seemingly unnecessary miles. It does mean that I am
not to struggle as the Master's bondslave. God has allowed this to
come to me, and I can trust Him the rest of the way. God has
allowed me to give up my coat so I am willing to trust Him with
my cloak. He has allowed me to be compelled to go one mile so I
can trust Him to help me go two. He has allowed me to be hit on
the right side so I can trust Him for the left side. As a bondslave I
am to see that the Master has allowed this to come: therefore I
will rejoice, praise Him, thank Him, and seek not to quench the
Spirit's quarry work.

If you will study closely the Bible accounts from early church
history, as well as some today, you'll have to admit that this view
of God's will is a distinctive mark of those who understand the
servant's life. Silas understood this in the jail. Daniel apparently
understood it in the lions' den. Shadrach, Meshach, and Abed-
nego undoubtedly understood it in the fiery furnace. And certainly Job had grasped this view when he said, "Though he slay
me, yet will I trust in him (Job 13:15).

It could not be more clearly seen than in the life of Paul as he
clarified his vision about the thorn in the flesh. When you read
2 Corinthians 12:7-10, you understand Paul acknowledged that
God had allowed Satan to do this (the same as with Job and his
trials and with Jesus and His temptations). Paul also had received

the thorn and was rejoicing in it as (v. 9) he testified he derived great pleasure from it (v. 10). Second Corinthians 6:1-10 further magnifies the strength that is inherent in the bondslave's life as Paul viewed the circumstances of life as God's allowed will.

When we struggle against God's allowed will it appears that we can expect the same calamities as did Peter in cutting off the ear of the high priest's servant and Jonah rerouted by the great fish.

To receive and rejoice in God's allowed will for myself in every situation of life does not relieve me from seeking God's perfect will. On the contrary, I will pray, praise, ask, knock, seek, work, sacrifice, claim, and search moment by moment for God's perfect will. However, once I have committed myself to such hungering and thirsting after God's will, then I will be ready to receive all that comes to me in life as the allowed will of God which becomes then God's perfect will for my life. At such a point I have every scriptural reason to expect to be satisfied and shaped for all eternity (Matt. 5:6).

We can never enter into the joy of experiencing God's will until we are God's children through salvation. This view of life and its circumstances is reserved only for those that are "in Christ." Even after we are saved, we will never be able to rejoice fully in life until we, as bondslaves, view all of life's circumstances as God's allowed will, preparing us to coreign with Him throughout eternity!

16 | Dangers

Moreover he must have a good report of them which are without; lest he fall into reproach and the snare of the devil (1 Tim. 3:7).

There are dangers to being a servant. What would you think they might be—overwork, misuse, abuse? No, these are not the dangers because the bondslave of Christ has a good Master. The danger of the believer in Christ is being deceived about the servant life and thereby missing the joy, blessing, usefulness, and eternal rewards of such a life. Here are some subtle snares that Satan seems to use to snag the would-be servant.

1. *Lack of Mastery:* The true bondslave of Christ must be mastered in all areas of his life. If one area is absent from underneath this mastery, then there is little hope of being a bondslave. Our attitude toward material things must be mastered by Christ. Matthew 6:24 makes that plain. We must see ourselves as stewards, not as owners. When the Master says give, we give; lie down, we lie down. Don't acquire—we do not acquire. Whatever the Master says about material things, we do. The area of mastery over material things is difficult, but many will find it easier in this area than some others. Do not allow the enemy to say, "A servant is to be mastered only at one point or another." No, there is to be no attitude unmastered. We are either mastered wholly or we are wholly unmastered.

2. *Wrong Inward Attitudes:* The Bible says "Whatsoever things are true, . . . honest, . . . just, . . . pure, . . . of good report, think on these things" (Phil. 4:8). That's speaking of the inward attitude. Some people, as we look at them on the outside, seem to be giving, sharing, or passive servant-type people. But many times on the inside these people are filled with envy, jealousy, suspicion, and distrust. The inward attitude must be mastered, as well as any other attitude.

   An account is given concerning Reece Howell on this very danger. One evening he and his friend were speaking in the open air, the friend speaking first. The Holy Ghost so used his friend that Howell began to wonder how he would ever preach following him (Howell was not a gifted open-air speaker). That grew into a thought of jealousy. "No one knew it," he confessed, "but that night the Holy Ghost whipped me and humbled me to the dust. He showed me the ugliness of jealousy and how the devil would take advantage of such a thing to damage the souls of those people. I never saw a thing I hated more than that, and I could have cursed myself for it. The Holy Ghost spoke to my heart, 'Didn't you come out to the open air for these souls to be blessed, and what difference does it make through whom I bless them?' He told me to confess the sin to my friend, and if ever He found it in me again, I would have to make a public confession. From that day on I have not dared to cherish a thought of jealousy, because not once did the Holy Ghost go back on His word to me. Whatever warning of punishment He had given me, if I disobeyed, I had to pay the full penalty. A person might think it was a life of bondage and fear. It would be to the flesh, but to the new man in Christ it was a life of fullest liberty."[1]

3. *Judging Others:* This is illustrated clearly with Mary and Martha (Luke 10:38-42). How we want to defend dear Martha. We are aware of how she feels. We often want to

complain, "Why should I be a servant when others couldn't care less" or "I'm not going to serve if others intend to lord it over me." We find ourselves with the same attitude as Peter when Jesus called on him to serve. "Lord, and what shall this man do?" (John 21:21). Someone gave me a devotional reading that really drove this point home.

But how like most of us Peter was. He wanted to evaluate John's assignment before he accepted his own. Would John be given a higher position, a better title, greater opportunities? How often we miss our sublime, unique calling from Christ when we compare ourselves with others. How often the cultural standards of value in positions, power, salaries, size of office or home, and material possessions beguile us, and we are blinded, unable to comprehend what has been entrusted to us.

Comparisons lead us to competition; competition leads to consternation. We muddle and then meddle with others and their lives. And the Master says, "Claim what I've given you, assume your calling, and get moving. Never mind what I'm giving to or doing with others. *You* follow Me!"

The challenge is to remove your eyes from others and to choose for oneself the bondslave life! It is not our concern to impose the servant's life upon others or to judge others' servanthood or to delay our becoming a servant because of what others may do. While it is true that we are to make disciples, it is equally true that people cannot be made to be a disciple or servant. You cannot force others to do spiritual things. It is our place to "make" ourselves bondslaves and leave those about us to the Lord. "But made himself of no reputation, and took upon him the form of a servant, and was made in the likeness of men" (Phil. 2:7). "For though I be free from all men, yet have I made myself servant unto all, that I might gain the more" (1 Cor. 9:19).

4. *Looking but Not Living:* Another danger is looking like but not living like a servant. This is probably the most subtle of

all Satan's snares. Do not try to *look* like a servant! Commit and purpose to *live* the servant life inside, and then you will find that God will be able to take care of how you look outside.

Do not serve to draw attention to yourself or to satisfy yourself. The moment one begins to do this there is one fact for certain—that person ceases to be a bondslave and becomes a man pleaser! Either he is trying to please himself or another person. Clearly at such a moment it is impossible for us to be the *doulos* of Christ because Galatians 1:10 declares, "For do I now persuade men or God? or do I seek to please men? for if I yet pleased men, I should not be the servant of Christ." Jesus made Himself a servant, poor and without reputation (Phil. 2:7-8) not to:

(1) create a dramatic show in order to attract people;
(2) to impress the world with sensationalism;
(3) to prove to Himself that He could do it.

Not at all. He made Himself a servant, not for looks but to glorify the Father and enrich others with the gospel. Not looks for men but living for the Master!

We must also understand that the *servant* is the one who is indwelled, *not the service.* It is true that we will be judged and rewarded by our works. What kind of works? Good works. Good works are those done by the servant who is indwelled and anointed in submission to the Master. The church and the kingdom do not need more organization endowed with enthusiasm but rather organization indwelled by Holy Spirit-anointed servants. Whatever deficiency exists in Christian service today is not due to the message but to the messenger. So, live the life of a servant. Forget about the looks.

5. *Lack of Language:* Another factor that is a danger for the servant is lack of language. The language of the servant is prayer. Luke 18:1 states "that men ought always to pray, and not to faint." We will see this more clearly when we next study the language of the servant, but it is vitally im-

portant that those who seek to live the servant life understand that it is absolutely impossible to do so if we lack the language of the servant. But herein is the danger because Satan will minimize what the servant must maximize!

6. *Shortcut Servants:* The next danger that often snags servants is that they desire to become "sudden servants." Exodus 21:1-6 indicates that the bondslave way is a lifelong commitment. The commitment at the doorpost may be a momentary experience, but still there is a life of conforming that is needful and lies ahead. A believer should not expect a "quick fix" to becoming a bondslave. This is not an excuse for spiritual abnormality and stunted spiritual growth, as is seen among many believers today. Rather, it is to understand that the bondslave life is one of *growing* in maturity.

I do believe the Master is desirous for us to abide as a bondslave the very moment we become His at salvation.

It also seems that most believers move away from a bondslave life commitment. For some, the *doulos* life seems to come quicker than with others. Most of us will find it is a journey that takes time and comes inch by inch, not acre by acre. The Lord has dealt with me on the smallest of matters. Often they have been nits I thought I had already yielded. It is amazing how such a tiny thing can weight us down. But when released, the buoyancy of the soul makes it seem as if the load were a trillion tons. Oh, what a glorious relief and release that is! What a shame that Satan can use such tiny things to crush us and keep us from being Jesus' beloved servant. "Lay aside *every weight*, and the sin which doth so easily beset us, and let us run with patience the race that is set before us" (Heb. 12:1).

One who grasped the servant life wrote that one of the Lord's purposes for the experiences of his life was to transform him into a servant:

The Holy Ghost took me through grade after grade. The process of changing one's nature (replacing self-nature by the divine nature) was very slow and bitter. It was a daily dying and showing forth the life of Christ, but that life was the life of a victim. Christ was the greatest Victim this side of the cross, the greatest Victor on the other; and the daily path was the way of the cross: every selfish motive and every selfish thought was at once dealt with by the Holy Spirit. In my boyhood days the strictest man I knew was my school master, but how often I said the Holy Spirit was a thousand times more strict—the school master could only judge by actions, but the Holy Ghost was judging by the motive."[2]

The enemy will try to snatch you away or distract you from the path of the servant's life by saying, "You see, such a life is just impossible to live—you've tried it for a month, six months, a year. Give up! Settle back into comfortable spiritual childhood along with most of the church." But the bondslave must know that such talk is from the enemy himself and represents the most acute danger to the most joyous life for the believer. At such times of danger let us claim again the help of:

(1) Ephesians 6:16: Above all, taking the shield of faith, where-with ye shall be able to quench all the fiery darts of the wicked.
(2) Hebrews 10:38: Now the just shall live by faith: but if any man draw back, my soul shall have no pleasure in him.
(3) Philippians 3:15: Let us therefore, as many as be perfect, be thus minded: and if in any thing ye be otherwise minded, God shall reveal even this unto you.

Herein is the danger: Satan will minimize what a servant is to maximize.

17 | LANGUAGE

Prayer

And he spake a parable unto them to this end, that men ought always to pray, and not to faint (Luke 18:1).

God has chosen to work through prayer and even to limit Himself to prayer. The Master will even let work go undone if the servant refuses to respond in the language of prayer. *Prayer is everything for everything!* It is the verbal and nonverbal language of love between the servant and his Master.

Prayer is when a burden from God is placed upon His Spirit dwelling within the believer, which, in turn, generates conversation between that believer and the throne of God, via Christ, in order that the believer will serve and intercede well-pleasingly to the will of God. Julian of Norwich articulated the depth of such God-originated communication: "I am the Ground of thy beseeching: first it is My will that thou have it; and after, I make thee to will it; and after, I make thee to beseech it and thou beseechest it. How should it then be that thou shouldst not have thy beseeching?"[3] (In this light it is easy to recognize how essential that all facets of our lives be controlled by the indwelling Spirit so nothing will lack the burden of God and our well-pleasing response.)

What kind of language does the "doulos" servant speak? It is the language of prayer! What follows is not a "how-to" lesson but an "ought-to" lesson. Our prayer should be, "Dear Lord, may we fall under, be brought under, or have placed upon us the great burden of joy for prayer!"

We need to know who God is, who we are, what's going on, and how critical the prayer language of the servant is to it all. There is a God in heaven, with an all-sufficient supply for all of our needs. There is a church on earth, with a wondrous calling for here and hereafter. Then there is prayer for the servant, waiting to bring both God and the church together! Do you realize how helpless we are if our lines of communication are cut? In war, thousands of people have died because the enemy was allowed to break down or cut lines of communication.

My unit in Vietnam had some unusual missions that required a good deal of isolation from other larger forces. Consequently, I always had at least three radio operators with me among my twenty-eight men. I quickly learned that the enemy's first target was to kill or knock out the radio man and thereby cut our lines of communication which linked us to help, reinforcements, and supplies. Predictably, I, like many others, learned quickly to ensure that our means of communication were carefully protected because the enemy had us in a pitifully helpless position without that critical connection.

The *doulos* servant is also helpless if he does not *learn* the language of prayer, *use* the language of prayer, and *keep* the lines of that language open. This will be one of the toughest parts of your life as a servant. It will be a constant war to keep the enemy from destroying your vital line of communication with the Father (Eph. 6:18; Gal. 6:9; Luke 18:1).

Caution! When many see the subject of prayer they begin to think thoughts like, *I've heard about prayer before; we have prayer in our home. We have the blessing at meals, and we have prayer when we go to bed. We pray when we get ready to go on a trip.* It certainly is true that this is prayer, but so often this sort of praying and our entire personal prayer life become casual and careless. Lackadaisical handling of such a holy practice as conversation and communion with God is truly dangerous, even to a blessed and prospering servant.

This danger is graphically illustrated in 2 Chronicles 26:15-21 where King Uzziah was stricken with disease and death because of careless and casual use of holy things! The verses prior to this section make it clear that the king was being mightily blessed, but in the midst of that blessing he became presumptuous, arrogant, and careless with the things of God. Because of such an attitude and action he was smitten by God with a dread disease. He was thrown out of the holy place of God, was placed on the sideline, and on the shelf. After losing his place he was replaced by another. How searching and gripping this is! I am certain that many of our Christian difficulties have resulted because we have been casual and careless with our communication with a holy God. We truly need to be smitten by God, but it needs to be with the power like Elijah on Mount Carmel, Moses at the Red Sea, and many others who committed themselves to the servant's life and learned the servant's language.

When the servant, Joshua, entered into communication with the Lord by asking, "What saith my Lord unto his servant?" it was declared to Joshua that conversation with the Lord was, in fact, such "holy ground" that the servant's shoes should be removed! (Josh. 5:12-15). Do we see that when we speak of prayer we are talking about a "holy hotline" to the power source of all the universe? We want to be careful not to lose it, misuse it, or abuse it—but, instead, use it. Does it dawn on you that the most seemingly insignificant servant holds the key to a life of effective service here on earth to stand against the forces of hell and then to share as a coreigner with Christ throughout eternity? Dear servant of Christ, you have the key—prayer. Use it, use it, use it!

Any attempt to serve without the servant language of prayer is like attempting to swim with no water or to eat with no food or to breathe with no air. It would all be nothing but foolishness! If I have no air I will not breathe. If I have a little air I will do a little breathing. If I have no prayer I will do no service that is acceptable. If I have little prayer I will do little acceptable service.

The importance of the servant's use of the language of prayer has numerous examples. Jesus, the Servant, prayed, needing heavenly communication and counsel before He entered His larger work of His first Galilean tour (Mark 1:35).

The apostles' lives of service were marked by regular rendezvous with the Lord. They "gathered themselves together unto Jesus" (Mark 6:30). Also, when Jesus chose His servants it was His desire that He and they be in contact with one another, "that they should be with him" (Mark 3:13-21). In fact, these powerful servants of Christ became so close to Him that He declared, "I call you not servants . . . but I have called you friends" (John 15:15). They indeed were servants, but they were so close to the Lord that He called these servants "friends." (Jesus was a Servant but was called by His Father, "Son.") The servant life is one of close contact, communion, and communication which is totally impossible without the language of prayer.

In recent generations this same truth has been made clear through the lives of John Wesley, Praying Hyde, Reece Howell, David Brainard, George Muller, and so many who have been associated with great spiritual awakenings. All of these understood how absolutely essential and inseparable the servant life and the language of prayer are to each other.

How logical all this is! How can one serve well if one has little or no conversation or communion with his Master? We will serve effectively only in direct proportion to our praying. Prayer is the language that links the bondslave to dependency on the Master. Prayer is far more than most of us think or see. We have such a shallow view of prayer, when we see this language as only some sort of magical method by which we will get "stuff" for ourselves, family, friends, and churches. We must see how much more this language really is. What many call prayer, I'm convinced does very little. But the kind of praying that God blesses is the right kind of praying by the right kind of people.

God has chosen the servant and the servant's language/prayer in order to:

1. get things done here on earth;
2. get us ready to coreign through eternity.

Prayer was included in your salvation. It gives you *service* which is anointed and acceptable; it is what provides power for you to *stand* against Satan; and it allows you to *share* a throne in eternity as coruler. Prayer is "everything for everything!" It causes to happen that which God has already decided and willed. It has been noted "that we can do more than pray but we cannot do more than pray until we have prayed." How true that is. So few are saved (Matt. 7:13-14). Even fewer commit themselves to the *doulos* life. Fewer still understand and learn the servant's language of prayer.

There are three things that are absolutely and inseparably linked. These are: prayer life, servant life, and coreigning life. This is a most glorious and divine connection. Consider this: if greatness in heaven is determined by our servant life here, and if our servant life here is determined by communication through prayer, then we must recognize that prayer now is basic even for our ministry throughout eternity.

Do you think prayer will stop once we arrive in heaven? Of course not, it is the language of communication between the servant and Master, who are deeply in love with each other. Does the bride stop talking to the groom after the wedding? No, and neither will we after the marriage supper of the Lamb. You see how important it is to learn here and now to communicate before eternity, because the marriage is to last forever. Further it is unthinkable, to me, that God would entrust coreigning and coruling throughout all eternity to one who, while here on earth, would not talk, ask, consult, commune, communicate, or counsel with Him about these passing, temporal affairs, but instead was rather careless, casual, self-centered, and often rebellious to the will of the Master. In my opinion, such an ideal is not logical, theological, or even eschatalogical. There is no tolerance in heaven for selfishness, self-centeredness, and rebellion. (Hell will house Lucifer and the fallen angels to prove exactly that point.) God desires and looks for believers who will serve here while in constant contact, conversation, and communion through the language of prayer, so God may have them as coreigners and corulers forever.

This stewardship of communication is part of the substance where our Master speaks, "Well done, thou good and faithful servant: thou hast been faithful over a few things, I will make thee ruler over many things: enter thou into the joy of thy lord" (Matt. 25: 21).

You may protest, "I don't know how to pray." Well, just open your heart and your mouth, and God will help and teach you to pray. To me prayer is like mail from a loved one. The concern is not with the stationery or even the grammar. What counts is the contents of the heart. John Bunyan said, "It is better to have a heart without words than words without heart."

"Lord, teach us to pray" (Luke 11:1).

Praise

And they, continuing daily with one accord in the temple, and breaking bread from house to house, did eat their meat with gladness and singleness of heart, Praising God, and having favor with all the people. And the Lord added to the church daily such as should be saved (Acts 2:46-47).

If you have ever heard a true servant pray you will have been able to recognize the distinctive dialect of intercession, silence, and praise. What is praise? Praise is to commend worth, to express approval, to laud, to give commendation and glory. In today's jargon, it is to brag. While "thanksgiving" deals with *what* God does, "praise" deals with *who* God is. But both are inseparably woven together, and the entire Bible is flooded with both praise and thanksgiving.

Praise is a servant's personal and special gift to God. There is a question in Psalm 116:12, "What shall I render unto the Lord for all his benefits toward me?" The answer comes in verses 16 and 17, "O Lord, truly I am thy servant; I am thy servant, and the son of thine handmaid: thou hast loosed my bonds. I will offer to thee the sacrifice of thanksgiving, and will call upon the name of the Lord."

What does praise do? Praise speaks. Praise speaks loudly and clearly to both the seen and the unseen. Of course, it speaks because praise is part of a language. Praise is so critical to the servant life that David appointed an army of four thousand just to praise God (1 Chron. 23:5,30). It has been pointed out that this was one of David's last official acts before his death. Therefore, it should be significant to note, that of all the triumphs and trage- dies of this great servant's life, one of the greatest triumphs came, when at the end of his life, he had learned the importance and cruciality of praise before God. The sooner we learn this, the better.

Here is an account from the life of John "Praying" Hyde.

> I remember John telling me that in those days, if on any day four souls were not brought into the fold, at night there would be such a weight on his heart that it was positively painful, and he could not eat nor sleep. Then, in prayer he would ask his Lord to show him what was the obstacle in him to this blessing. He invariably found that it was the want of praise in his life. This command, which has been repeated in God's Word hundreds of times—surely it is all important! He would then confess his sin, and accept the forgiveness by the Blood. Then he would ask for the spirit of praise as for any other gift of God. So he would exchange his ashes for Christ's garland, his mourning for Christ's oil of joy, his spirit of heaviness for Christ's garment of praise (the Song of the Lamb—praising God beforehand for what He was going to do), and as he praised God souls would come to him, and the numbers lacking would be made up.[4]

Hyde considered praise one of the great secrets to his powerful spiritual life.

What Does Praise Say?

1. *Praise tells the Master* that we are honored and privileged to serve You! If we were called to be an ambassador of this country to some other nation we would think of that as an

honor and a privilege. It is all the more an honor to be a servant of God Almighty. The servant will find himself spending much time praising his Master for the good "job" he is allowed to hold. Think of it—to belong to the household of God, to be chosen by God Almighty to be a co-laborer, to be a partner, to be an intercessor, to be backed by the power and authority of the God of the universe. Think of all that, and you undoubtedly will praise Him!

2. *Praise tells heaven* that we servants are depending upon God in heaven! God's servants *must* have help from heaven. Praise is lifting God's name up unashamedly. Sometimes the church is accused of trying to "work up" praise. The larger problem today is not that the church is trying to work up praise but that it is throwing it out. In America we are moving posthaste to banish the names to be praised, that of God and Jesus. It has become a literal crime to praise God as a nation. What our nation is now saying is, "We no longer need God and heaven's help." No nation has ever survived while turning its back on God. And no believer will either! We need to praise Him so heaven will know that we depend upon God and His resources.

3. *Praise tells the world* to whom we belong! "O give thanks unto the Lord, for he is good: for his mercy endureth forever. Let the redeemed of the Lord say so, whom he hath redeemed from the hand of the enemy" (Ps. 107:1-2). You remember 1 Chronicles 23:30 where the nation of Israel was telling the world, morning and night, to whom they belonged! When we stand before God in eternity the sweetest name that can pass our lips will be the name of Jesus. That is exactly why I believe that you will find the distinctive dialect of praise on the servant's lips here and now when he prays and speaks.

4. *Praise tells doubts* that we are free! (Matt. 14:24-33). Doubts come from fear. Fear comes from a lack of faith in the Lord. Lack of faith comes from self-dependency.

Sooner or later all of us find out that "self" isn't able to do all that we thought it could. Praise puts God up front and puts self behind. Paul Billheimer says that praise produces forgetfulness of self and that's good health. Praise casts out defensiveness, hostility, irritation, sulking, all of which center in self. Praise raises us beyond self. Praise is the spark plug of faith. It causes our faith to become airborne and rise above our doubts, fears, and ourselves. Praise is the detergent that washes out self-doubt. Praise frees us to get loose and serve and intercede in the power of God. Praise Him!

5. *Praise tells fellow servants* "keep your helmet on straight!" I am referring to the study on the helmet and the full armor of God. A good example of one servant encouraging another is Elijah at Dothan. Elijah, upon keeping his mind, attention, and eyesight on the Lord, was able to encourage his fellow servant. We will either encourage or discourage the saints.

6. *Praise tells the devil* to flee! "Resist the devil, and he will flee from you" (Jas. 4:7). One of the clearest illustrations of this is in 2 Chronicles 20:20-23. The enemies of God's people are caught in "ambushments" because of the people's praise. The devil and his crowd were put on the run when the praises of God's people called down heaven's help. A clear New Testament example was what happened after Paul and Silas began to praise the Lord in Acts 16:24-36. Praise confuses both the seen and the unseen enemy. Praise attracts heaven and repels the devil.

7. *Praise tells us* to be at peace! Peace will surely come if we have told the Master how honored we are to serve Him. Tell heaven how much we are depending upon it. Tell doubt that we are free. Tell servants to be encouraged. Tell the world to whom we belong. Tell the devil to flee. Then, there is no way to keep from having peace in our hearts after such a series of praise. Remember, we have Jesus. That is truth. We have righteousness. That is grace. Jesus

plus righteousness equals peace. Peace should be the servant's constant state of heart.

How Do We Praise the Lord?

It is not merely in music, and it is not just an emotional experience, but it is based upon who God is. It is not necessary to raise the hands or even to raise the voice, both of which are scriptural but not necessary. "By him therefore let us offer the sacrifice of praise to God continually, that is, the fruit of our lips giving thanks to his name. But to do good and to communicate forget not: for with such sacrifices God is well pleased" (Heb. 13:15-16).

This text clearly shows us that praise is: *a sacrifice* (put self to death); *a spoken language*. While praise does not necessarily have to be voiced aloud there is something special about verbally expressed praise. It is the fruit of the lips. One of the greatest needs today is to establish an atmosphere of praise, as it says in the text, "continually."

This is to begin in our hearts, extending to our homes, work, schools, and churches. A significant commitment would be to establish an atmosphere of praise from within and extending it to the sphere in which we find ourselves to the glory of God and to the defeat of Satan, so we might serve and intercede more pleasingly for our Master. Praise is part of prayer's distinctive dialect which is vital to the servant's life.

Silence

Behold, I am vile; what shall I answer thee? I will lay mine hand upon my mouth (Job 40:4).

Be silent, O all flesh, before the Lord: for he is raised up out of his holy habitation (Zech. 2:13).

Therefore Eli said unto Samuel, Go, lie down: and it shall be, if he call thee, that thou shalt say, Speak, Lord; for thy servant heareth. So Samuel went and lay down in his place. And the Lord came, and stood, and called as at other times, Samuel,

Samuel. Then Samuel answered, Speak; for thy servant heareth (1 Sam. 3:9-10).

Another of the distinctive dialects of the servant's language is silence. Silence is one of the most important and beautiful "sounds" of the servant's language. It is essential to the servant/intercessor's life and language. True conversation always has two sides, the speaker's and the listener's. Both people in the conversation do both!

And so it is with conversation of the servant with the Master! The secret of "spiritual silence" is to allow ourselves to hear God as He speaks to us. How logical and fitting this is for the servant to be silent and listen to his Master for guidance, commendation, counsel, and correction. How illogical, unbecoming, and ill-mannered it would be for a servant to do most of the talking. After all, who knows the most and who is giving the instructions anyway? Prayer, then, is not telling God what to do but to understand what God wants us to do. Do not misunderstand, I am not speaking of "silent prayer" but "silent silence" where the servant is simply silent and listens to the Master.

Silence Honors God—"Be not rash with thy mouth, and let not thine heart be hasty to utter anything before God: for God is in heaven, and thou upon earth: therefore let thy words be few" (Eccl. 5:2). "Be silent, O all flesh, before the Lord: for he is raised up out of his holy habitation" (Zech. 2:13).

Silence honors God by showing respect and reverence. What a joy it is for a servant to sit, to stand, to kneel quietly and silently in the presence of his Master!

Silence Allows Us to Hear God—"Behold, I am vile; what shall I answer thee? I will lay mine hand upon my mouth" (Job 40:4). "Be still, and know that I am God: I will be exalted among the heathen, I will be exalted in the earth" (Ps. 46:10).

If we will be still and silent before God we will know that He is God. In hospitals and during tragedies, we are reduced to doing nothing but sitting and listening. At those times we seem to hear God speak the loudest in our spirit. When we are silent we will hear God by His Word. When we are silent we will hear God even by His whisper. One paraphrase calls this God's "gentle whispers" (1 Kings 19:12, TLB). Again, do not misunderstand, I do not mean that God is necessarily going to speak to us aloud. God has never spoken to me personally aloud. Frankly, if He did it would probably scare me to death! But God does incline one's heart, and He does speak to us in an unmistakable manner. We may test what we hear to see if it agrees with the Bible, with Christ's life, with our servant calling, and with bringing glory to God. Does it bring salvation? Does it equip the saints? Does it draw us closer to Jesus? Such questions will ensure that what we have heard has truly been from the Lord.

Silence Must Be Practiced—We are probably all alike at this point. We had rather talk than listen, so we must practice to be silent. "But let it be the hidden man of the heart, in that which is not corruptible, even the ornament of a meek and quiet spirit, which is in the sight of God of great price" (1 Pet. 3:4). "And that ye study to be quiet, and to do your own business and to work with your own hands, as we commanded you" (1 Thess. 4:11). After the apostle Paul was converted he asked, "Lord, what wilt thou have me to do?" Immediately God sent him into solitary confinement (Acts 9:6) so God might have his undivided attention. As Paul listened, God spoke. Paul became the servant/intercessor that God desired to use.

Richard Wurmbrand said something to this effect, "An open mouth is to the insides of a Christian what an open door is to a warm house in the winter." To be sure, we must be opening our mouths, witnessing, praying, and engaged in other ministries, but it is also true that we must learn to close our mouth and be silent in order that God might speak and our soul might burn for Him. Another writer reminds us, "The one fact we forget is that the saints of old were capable of spiritual silence simply because they had not contracted our modern habit of ceaseless talk in their ordinary life. Their days were days of silence, relieved by periods of conversation, while our days are a wilderness of talk with a rare oasis of silence."

"The Lord spake unto Moses face to face, as a man speaketh unto his friend" (Ex. 33:11).

Silence! Silence! Silence!
God is Speaking! Honor Him! Hear Him!

Intercession

Likewise the Spirit also helpeth our infirmities: for we know not what we should pray for as we ought: but the Spirit itself maketh intercession for us with groanings which cannot be uttered. And he that searcheth the hearts knoweth what is the mind of the Spirit, because he maketh intercession for the saints according to the will of God (Rom. 8:26-27).

The servant ought to pray (see Luke 18:1). The servant must pray because it is impossible to serve pleasingly without conversation with the Master. Praying then is the "servant's language." But how does this servant language sound? It seems that each language has a distinctive dialect. A dialect is a form of spoken language peculiar to a community, social group, or an occupational group. What is the peculiar sound of this spiritual occupational group called *douloi?* To be sure the servant language of prayer consists of many sounds—confession, adoration, supplication, petition, and so forth. However, one can most easily discern a servant's language by its distinctive dialect of intercession, praise, and silence.

What Is Intercession?

What is intercession? Some people claim that all praying is intercession. But praying is not all intercession. It seems that the Bible has a more pointed definition of intercession in light of the servant's life. Most basically an intercessor is a "go-between." Abraham interceded for Sodom (Gen. 18:22ff.). Paul interceded for the Jewish people (Rom. 9:1-3). And Moses interceded for a nation. These were people standing in the gap between man's needs and God. Please do not misunderstand. This is not referring to some priest who must come between God and man for spiritual needs, but rather a fellow believer who comes to help and share the burden of another.

Jesus is the greatest go-between (John 3:17; Matt. 20:28; 1 Tim. 2:5; Heb. 12:24; Heb. 7:25). Jesus' life was as a servant, completely devoted to "interceding." He came from heaven to intercede. His entire earthly ministry was one of intercession. When He found the hungry, the sick, the guilty, the lonely, the broken, the hated, the lost, the wicked, and even the dead, He always devoted himself to interceding for them. We must not forget that Jesus is still the same "yesterday, today, and forever" (Heb. 13:8). "Wherefore he is able also to save them to the uttermost that come unto God by him, seeing he ever liveth to make intercession for them" (Heb. 7:25). Here is how this same Jesus ministers at the point of intercession.

1. Jesus in *person* intercedes *for us.* "Who is he that condemneth? It is Christ that died, yea rather, that is risen again, . . . who also maketh intercession for us" (Rom. 8:34).

2. Jesus in *Spirit* intercedes *with us* and *through us.* "And he that searcheth the hearts knoweth what is the mind of the Spirit, because he maketh intercession for the saints according to the will of God" (Rom. 8:27).

For us—helping *our* infirmities (Rom. 8:26). *Through us—* helping *others'* infirmities, "For as many as are led by the Spirit of God, they are the sons of God" (v. 14). This servant life is to help others. Intercession is helping others. Jesus is the perfect example of the servant/intercessor! It is obvious that the servant life and the intercessory life are one and the same! A true servant is an intercessor, and a true intercessor is a servant! Therefore, let us refer to the *doulos* bondslave as the servant/intercessor.

The Worst Hurt—The Best Help

The spirit also helpeth our infirmities (Rom. 8:26).

What is the worst possible physical infirmity? Of course, it is physical death. But there is an infirmity far worse than physical death—that is spiritual death. The basic purpose of all of Christ's intercession is to help to intercede at the point of our worst infirmity, spiritual death. That is also the basic purpose of the believer's intercession, the purpose of all intercession! The ministry of intercession is to point people to the Father who loves them and desires to be their everlasting Companion. Consequently, any true intercessory life or servant life will have a heavy burden for the unsaved and will be interceding and helping in order to win them to Christ.

How will the servant intercede? The servant will intercede by prayer and by participation. That is by both lip and life.

By Prayer

> I exhort therefore, that, first of all, supplications, prayers, intercessions, and giving of thanks, be made for all men; I will therefore that men pray everywhere, lifting up holy hands, without wrath and doubting (1 Tim. 2:1,8).

Prayer and "intercession" are so connected to each other that the same word is used for both in 1 Timothy 2:1 and 4:5. Intercessory prayer is laying aside our own personal needs and desires in order to step in and to help others without a concern to please ourselves. "We then that are strong ought to bear the infirmities of the weak, and not to please ourselves (Rom. 15:1).

> If radio's slim fingers can pluck melody from the night, and
>   toss it over a continent or sea,
> If petaled white notes of a violin are blown across a mountain
>   or a city's din;
> If sounds, like crimson roses are culled from the blue air.
> Why should mortals wonder if God hears prayer?
> —Author unknown

If we find ourselves praying more for personal possessions for those nearest us than we are praying for people who need us, then we have an indication of our lack of the true servant/intercessor life.

Prayer coordinator T. W. Hunt of the Baptist Sunday School

Board has filled four computer discs with prayers from the Bible and says, "Seven ninths of the prayers uttered by the great prayer warriors were answered by God because they were asking something on God's behalf. Two ninths of the prayers God answered were for personal things." Hunt, who keeps a list of his prayers and God's responses, said: "I have checked on my own prayer life and believe that it is in exactly the same proportions. When I was praying for the Kingdom, seven ninths were answered. When I was praying for something personal, two ninths were answered." The point of all this is that God is in agreement with intercession and intercessory prayer which is always "the distinctive dialect of the servant."

While intercession may only extend as far as prayer, it is often *more* than just prayers. Often when God sends a burden for intercessory prayer He also sends that same servant a burden for intercessory participation—physically.

Great prayer warriors declare that prayer intercession is the "heart of prayer" and that intercession is the highest and holiest level of praying. If this be so, and I believe it is, then does it not follow that intercessory *living* on the behalf of the servant is the highest and holiest level of living? I believe so! At such a point of praying, as well as living, the believer draws nearest to the life that Jesus exemplified.

It may be important to note that Romans 8:27 reminds us that our hearts are searched according to the will of God. Thus our willingness to participate physically in a call to intercession may be the point at which God determines if He will honor our prayers of intercession. One great intercessor came to this conclusion, "I am never to ask God to answer a prayer through others, if God could answer it through me." This intercessor and prayer warrior was saying, "I am willing to get involved—to participate!"

By Participation

After these things the Lord appointed other seventy also, and sent them two and two before his face into every city and place, whither he himself would come. Therefore said he unto them,

The harvest truly is great, but the laborers are few: pray ye therefore the Lord of the harvest, that he would send forth laborers into his harvest. Go your ways: behold, I send you forth as lambs among wolves. Carry neither purse, nor scrip, nor shoes: and salute no man by the way (Luke 10:1-4).

Participation means that we are involving our own flesh and blood—this is "hands-on" intercession. Let me attempt to bring together intercession through prayer that leads to intercession by physical participation.

The Steps to Intercession

The way of intercession follows along the path of exposure, burden, prayer, participation, and cost. As we follow these steps toward intercession compare them to Bible examples and see if they do not agree.

1. *Exposure.*—Jesus said in John 4:35: "Lift up your eyes and look on the fields." Before any intercession occurs we will be exposed to situations and people. This is why it is so critical for the believer to walk in God's will and to obey it immediately. We cannot do all but we are responsible for that to which we are led and exposed. The Lord sends each servant in different directions (Luke 10:1). It will help us to read Luke 4:25-27. We must understand that God will, out of all the people around us, lead us and expose us to those with whom He expects us to intercede. God has a marvelous plan! His plan is to scatter us all about to unique corners of the vineyard where He desires to touch lives and intercede.

   Each servant is to have the same impact—to win the lost. Perhaps you have said or heard said, "I don't want to hear or see that sort of thing," referring to a deep, troubling need of some sort. Such a response is the natural tendency, but the spiritual tendency of the servant is to be willing to be exposed to whatever the Spirit leads us.

2. *Burden.*—Paul declared that he had "great heaviness and continual sorrow" (Rom. 9:2). We may be assured, be-

cause Jesus lives in us to intercede (Heb. 7:25), that the Spirit will *lead* us, *expose* us, and *burden* us. Such a burden is the concern of the interceding Christ in us.

We may test our burden at this point whether it be from above or from below. The burden of Christ will always help people to glorify the Father that they may know Him, love Him, and follow Him. The length and depth of the burden may indicate the extent to which the Lord intends to use us in intercession, regardless of whether that intercession be by prayer only or by prayer and participation. We may be assured that if we respond positively to a God-given burden it will draw us away from or lessen our attraction to our own personal self-needs.

3. *Prayer.*—After the Spirit has led us, exposed us, and burdened us, we will find ourselves inescapably praying and thinking, and thinking, and thinking and praying. This burden of the Spirit will begin to brood upon us. It is my opinion that this is a signal that God Himself has already been burdened about this very item. When we are walking in the Spirit and will of God we do not pray in order to acquaint God with some burden about which He does not know but we are, in fact, being burdened *by God* to intercede through prayer. Once we begin to intercede by prayer we are in agreement with Jesus, the Servant/Intercessor. Look out, things are about to happen! Our ministry of intercession may end in prayer alone. It may be one prayer for one item or praying for a season, a year, or perhaps a lifetime for a certain burden.

4. *Participation.*—Intercessory prayer will most often call us to intercessory participation—to do something! "We then that are strong ought to bear the infirmities of the weak, and not to please ourselves" (Rom. 15:1). "Bear ye one another's burdens, and so fulfill the law of Christ" (Gal. 6:2). This participation could be a passing thing, such as buying someone a meal. It may be short-term or long-term. It even can be a lifetime calling to some specific min-

istry. Such interceding means bearing burdens as indicated in Galatians 6. *Whose* burdens will we bear? We will bear our own burdens, "Every man shall bear his own burden" (v. 5). We will bear "one another's burdens" (v. 2). We are to "do good unto all men, especially unto them who are of the household of faith" (v. 10). *Where* do we bear these burdens? The servant/intercessor will bear burdens at every opportunity (v. 10) as they are both presented and sought (2 Tim. 4:2, "in season, out of season"). *When* will we bear these burdens? We are to bear burdens "as we have, therefore opportunity (Gal. 6:10). Remember, this is "on-the-job training" here for life hereafter.

It is good for the servant/intercessor to bear burdens. Bearing others' burdens helps us to know better how to bear our own burdens, and it is an occasion to examine ourselves. Further, we find ourselves humbled when dealing with others' burdens and seemingly always thanking God for His grace.

5. *Cost.* —True God-given, Spirit-led, Christlike intercession will always cost. Expect it! Paul tells the cost of interceding under the burden of crosses (Gal. 6:17). Yes, intercession will cost you here but, dear friend, it will reward you there! (Matt. 20:26).

Why Intercede At All?

Intercession is to "help infirmities," not for self-gain. The true intercessor is a soul-winner interceding for the lost in order that they might escape spiritual death and have spiritual life. Further we intercede on behalf of the saved. Such intercession will also demonstrate to the world the love of God ("That they may know that we are His by how we love one another"). My opinion is that if we do not intercede in the name of Jesus we are only giving humanitarian aid which could be rendered by the most ungodly person. Humanitarian aid alone is far less than the believer has been saved and called to render. On the other hand, intervention becomes divine intercession when we are led by the Spirit, and we do so in Jesus' name. The Spirit of God produces fruit and gifts, both of which are to affect and enhance the interceding servant's life.

We intercede because we are to make ourselves a servant and that means intercession. Also, if the Perfect Servant/Intercessor is filling us we cannot help but intercede. We will intercede because this ministry is critical to the ultimate plan of God. God did not create the world and its inhabitants so they could fall and be lost in order that He would have to see His only beloved Son tortured and killed to save them. All that happened, but there is more.

God's ultimate plan is to have a kingdom that is filled with His love and those that love Him. That is why God interceded to save through His Servant Son. That is why God desires servants. That is why servants must pray. That is why praying must be intercessory! That is why intercessory prayers bring intercessory participation. That is why the life of the *doulos* bondslave must be one of intercession through prayer and participation. That is the distinctive dialect of the servant's prayer life—intercession! Do we speak it? Can it be heard by both lost and saved?

18 | BROKENNESS

The sacrifices of God are a broken spirit: a broken and a contrite heart, O God, thou wilt not despise (Ps. 51:17).

The Lord is nigh unto them that are of a broken heart; and saveth such as be of a contrite spirit (Ps. 34:18).

Whosoever shall fall upon that stone shall be broken; but on whomsoever it shall fall, it will grind him to powder (Luke 20:18).

For thus saith the high and lofty One that inhabiteth eternity, whose name is Holy; I dwell in the high and holy place, with him also that is of a contrite and humble spirit, to revive the spirit of the humble, and to revive the heart of the contrite ones (Isa. 57:15).

While Luke 20:18 really has a different meaning when applied to the context of the passage, to me it does have a message to the broken life of the believer. "Whosoever shall fall upon that stone shall be broken; but on whomsoever it shall fall, it will grind him to powder." It seems to indicate that if we are willing to fall voluntarily upon Christ, then we shall be victoriously broken. But if Christ must fall upon us then we'll be brought sorrowfully low. Someone has said, "The whole unbruised, unbroken man is of little use to God." That does not necessarily mean that the person is of no use at all, but he will be of little use. God has chosen to work through brokenness.

Ellice Hopkins put it beautifully,

Do you know the lovely fact about the opal? That, in the first place, it is made only of desert dust, sand, silica, and owes its beauty and preciousness to a defect. It is a stone with a broken heart. It is full of minute fissures which admit air and the air refracts the light. Hence, its lovely hues, and that sweet lamp of fire that ever burns at its heart; for the breath of the Lord God is in it.[5]

You're only conscious of the cracks and desert dust, but so He makes His precious opal. We must be broken in ourselves before we can give back the lovely hues of His light, and the lamp in the temple can burn in us and never go out.

The Blessings of Brokenness

"Brokenness" means to the unspiritual life of the flesh and the world "the end!" When a vase or a twenty-dollar bill is broken we say, "it's ruined, gone, ended!" But to the spiritual life brokenness means "the beginning!" Do not think of brokenness negatively. Do not be afraid of brokenness. Do not draw back from brokenness or its thought or teachings. Pray that the victory and joy of brokenness may be your craving, yearning, your life! To hold any other point of view is only to expose our lack of understanding and lack of oneness with Christ.

God is not trying to hide Himself, but God desires to reveal Himself (Heb. 1:1-2). God's desire to expose Himself is what brought Jesus down to sinful humanity via the manger, and Jesus continues to expose God today through redeemed man. Read 2 Corinthians 4:3-12 and discover the impact of this titanic truth. The treasure of God and Christ has been placed in earthen (breakable) vessels. These vessels (we) must be broken for the full glory and power of God to be exposed!

If, therefore, we expect to reveal Christ, we must break. He must have broken vessels! When the poor widow *broke* the seal of the little pot of oil and poured it forth, God multiplied it to pay her debts. Mary *broke* her beautiful alabaster box (rendering it henceforth useless), but the pent-up perfume filled the house. Jesus took the five loaves and *broke* them, and the bread multiplied sufficiently to feed 5,000. Jesus allowed His precious body to be *broken* by thorns, nails, and a spear, so that His inner life might be poured out for thirsty sinners to drink. The seal of Christ's tomb was *broken* to give the world, for all time, the witness of Christ's resurrection. A grain of wheat is *broken* up in the earth by death. God must have *broken* vessels! "Unbrokenness hides our treasure, the Lord Jesus Christ; only *BROKENNESS* will reveal Him!"[5] It is our hard shell of unbroken, sinful humanity that holds back the full flow of Christ's life through us.

Three biblical examples offer some profound lessons about brokenness that must be learned by the servant/intercessor.

Mary (John 12:1-8)

It is clear by Mary's actions that love is the basic motivation for brokenness. This is consistent with what we broke in the beginning: that the love of Christ is what compels us in this "foolish way." Brokenness is the result of a certain extravagance of love that refuses to count the personal cost. Think of it—a bottle of perfume, worth a workingman's pay for one year, with the top irreparably broken off and the contents poured out. In this action of brokenness there is no thought of return or of keeping any reserve for self. Such extravagant love!

There are two characters facing this moment of brokenness, Mary and Judas. One goes out a memorial; the other goes out a madman! Judas was galled not by the poor or the price but by the picture he saw. Judas saw extravagant, self-abandoning, unreserved love of a broken follower, and he saw how Jesus loved, blessed, and honored such a life so thoroughly given. Judas could not stand it because he knew he was not such a one. It should be a troubling thing to us believers if we fail to be broken and humble.

See how rich the rewards are of such extravagant love that leads to being broken and humbled at the feet of Jesus. While Mary was not invited to the feast of food, she shared in the most intimate way a spiritual feast with Jesus. She experienced, amid all the friends of Jesus and the festivities, what pleased Him most—the brokenness of an ordinary believer. Another rich reward was the fact that this act was to last forever and never to be forgotten (Matt. 26:13). Further, everyone in the house benefited from the sweet aroma of this broken and poured-out expression of Mary's extravagant love. What rich rewards are promised for a humble and broken life motivated by love of the Master!

Gideon (Judg. 7:16-21)

Gideon's broken pitchers seemed to be the key to blessing and power that accompany brokenness. Many of us like to hear our horns blown, but most of us hate to have our vessels broken. It is amazing how much the world and flesh can extract from people by blowing their horn. God intends to receive far, far more through man's brokenness. We must see in the account of Gideon's pitchers that refusing to break the vessel would have withheld the full force of God's blessing and power. The result of the unhidden glow and glory of God's full force coming from the broken pitcher was that a small band of God-obeying people became victorious over immeasurable odds (see vv. 12-21).

Jesus

Jesus makes a promise concerning brokenness. The promise of the cross is that the greatest breaking will bring the greatest blessing. Jesus said to His most intimate followers, "This is My blood shed for you and this is My body broken for you" (see Luke 22:19-20). Now the question comes, "Am I willing to be poured out and broken for the Lord, the lost, the saved, the family of God?" Jesus made it unmistakably clear how we should respond to His brokenness and spilledoutness. He said, "This do in remembrance of me [until I come again]" (v. 19). Communion with God is more than merely sipping juice and eating a crumb. It is being willing to be daily poured out and broken that Christ might be revealed in us until He comes for us!

So then, when extravagant love for our Master breaks us, we may expect His greatest blessings and power to be used in His servant/intercessor. The power to help others depends upon acceptance of a trampled life. Highways are open roads. Roads are not made for admiration, but for traffic. God breaks up the private life of his saints and makes it a thoroughfare for the world on one hand, and Himself on the other.

The Master's Mat

Blasted rock and broken stone,
    Ordinary earth,
Rolled and rammed and trampled
    on,
    Forgotten, nothing worth;
And blamed, but used day after
    day;
    An open road—the King's
    highway.
Often left outside the door,
    Sometimes in the rain,
Always lying on the floor,
    And made for mud and stain:
Men wipe their feet, and tread it flat,
    And beat it clean—the Master's
    mat.
Thou wast broken, left alone,
    Thou wast blamed, and worse,
Thou wast scourged and spat upon,
    Thou didst become my curse—
Lord Jesus, as I think of that
    I pray, make me Thy road, Thy
    mat.

—Author unknown[6]

God desires to break up "Private Drives" to make "Public Thoroughfare Streets" upon which souls will find Him!

The Cycle of Brokenness—Humility

Brokenness and humility are so close to each other that the words are interchangeable. However, they appear separate to me. The life of humility finds its beginning in a point of brokenness. Brokenness relates to a point in time whereas humility relates to a way of life. Brokenness relates to an experience and a decision whereas humility relates to an attitude, a spirit, an expression which is the result of such brokenness. We come to a point of brokenness, and the life we live from that point on should be humility.

This point of brokenness may or may not be a big "crisis" event or experience; however, sometimes, it is. Even if there is a "crisis" event we will still find a daily need for continual times of brokenness in order to maintain a life of humble living. I do not know a person having any one single crisis experience (after their salvation) that has been sufficient to keep them in a humble spirit of living year after year after year. But rather those humble servants I have known use every daily mundane trial and aggravation as an opportunity from God to be broken continually that they might continually live a humble life. A close look will reveal that a life of humility is one that moves from one point of brokenness to another point of brokenness, in between which is a life humbled before the Lord—hence, a daily cycle of broken humility.

To me this can be seen in the life of Christ as He was yielded to this cycle. See Him go aside to pray and be alone, then come forth in all humility. Such seems to be the daily occurrence of His Servant/Intercessor life. Christ in the garden of Gethsemane offers the perfect picture of this cycle. He was deeply yielded in a spirit of complete surrender under intense agony where sweat drops turned to blood. Then, in humility, He arose, went forth to live in the spirit, attitude, and expression of that brokenness. Never have we seen one as humble as He was, all the way to the cross!

A well-meaning friend told me, "Pastor, don't let this church break you!" Later, as I began to understand more the need for a broken and humbled life, I wrote in my personal notes the following:

Oh, dear Lord Jesus, may this very church *daily* offer me the challenges, adversities, demands, pressures, frustrations, calls, misunderstandings, through its ministry and people, that

I may see them as "God's gifts of grace," whereby I may have the opportunity constantly and daily to *choose* (not be forced) to be broken and humbled. May I see such as the "worm work" (Ps. 22:6-8) of God to keep me broken and humbled, just like You, dear, sweet Savior.

"Go *afresh* to Calvary. See Christ broken for me and come away willing to be broken for Thee!"

The point is this. After salvation we may have a big crisis experience that breaks us and ever reminds us of our need to be broken (Jacob's crippled hip is an example of this). Nonetheless, we will still find the need for a daily and constant choosing to be broken in order to live the humble, well-pleasing, servant life.

An observer watched curiously as two mountain goats headed toward each other on the same narrow, steep mountain path, one coming down and the other going up. As the two goats confronted each other and realized there was no possible way to pass, it looked as if there was going to be a struggle for the right of way. Then the strangest thing happened. The goat going uphill got down on his knees and bowed his head, and the goat coming down made his way over his back. Then the upward-bound goat arose from his knees and continued up the mountain. Remembering that story, I thought, *What a beautiful picture of the broken and humbled life*. Because, dear friend, the truth of it is in the spirit world: the way up is down—brokenness.

I heard of a rich farmer who had working for him a poor but very godly sharecropper. The rich, arrogant man ran into some difficulties, and having admired the humble, godly man's peace of mind in such difficult times, asked, "How in the world can I have such peace and victory as you in my hard times?"

The worker replied, "Well, Sir, you must get on your best clothes and go down to the old hog pen and dive into all the hog slop, muck, and mire until it's over your entire body. Then God will be able to give you peace and the victory you need."

The rich man was incensed and refused to do so. But matters became much worse in his personal life. Finally, one day he came to the worker with his best outfit of clothing on and confessed he was now ready to go to the hog pen. He would do whatever it took to have peace and victory. In that moment the godly worker made this profound statement, "Well, Sir, the truth of the matter is that you don't always have to go down to the hog pen, but you have to be *willing* to go to the hog pen before God can do anything with you."

God may or may not take us to the extremes that we may imagine. However, we may be certain of one truth: God will find out here on earth which of His children are willing to be broken, humble servants in order that He may have them coreign and corule for all eternity!

19 | HUMILITY

Whosoever therefore shall humble himself as this little child, the same is greatest in the kingdom of heaven (Matt. 18:4).

Blessed are the poor in spirit: for theirs is the kingdom of heaven (Matt. 5:3).

Notwithstanding in this rejoice not, that the spirits are subject unto you; but rather rejoice, because your names are written in heaven (Luke 10:20).

Humility is understanding who God is and who we are and then going about living our daily lives like we know those facts! Humility does not mean spiritlessness, weakness, cowardliness, or an inferiority complex but rather a life of high spiritual courage and strength. Humility is meekness, like a powerful animal that has been domesticated by its loving master. Such a life is loving, well-mannered, polite, behaved, gentle, trusting, and serving. It was said of Moses in Numbers 12:3, "Now the man Moses was very meek, above all the men which were upon the face of the earth." This is the sort of meek humility that takes off its shoes before God but is able to obey by standing up to the mightiest ruler of the land and declaring, "Thus saith the Lord!" James Boice describes this as one who can bow low before God to stand tall before men. Those who are truly humble have boldness because they know they have been touched by God and they have a message from Him.

142

Humility Asks an Action of Believers

Galatians 6:3 declares, "If someone thinks he is something when he really is nothing, he is only deceiving himself" (GNB). Paul says in Acts 20:19, "I came serving the Lord with all humility, many tears, and trials" (author's paraphrase). How do I serve in all humility? What action is required of me, the believer? What do these Scripture passages tell us about humility (Luke 18:14; 14:11; Matthew 23:12; 18:4; 2 Chronicles 7:14; 33:12; 1 Peter 5:5)? One obvious action is dictated—that is "to humble ourselves!"

However, some will not "humble themselves" and because of this lack of action must face the alternatives. What are the alternatives to "humbling self"?

1. *God Himself can humble us (Matt. 23:12; Luke 18:14; 14:11; Matt. 18:4).*—In fact, the Scriptures seem to promise that God will, in fact, humble us if we don't humble ourselves.

2. *God can allow others to humble us.*—In 2 Chronicles 33:11-13, Manasseh was humbled in just such a way. When God must humble us it is like having to twist someone's arm to get them to say, "I love you." If the love or humility must be squeezed out of someone, isn't there an emptiness to it? No wonder God desires us to humble ourselves!

3. *God can allow us to go unhumbled and unused.*—There are those who are unwilling to humble themselves, and even though God does humble them, they continue to refuse to live a submissive life. Instead they are rebellious, blame others, and become even harder, and, consequently, cannot be fully used of God.

4. *God can allow us to destroy ourselves due to the lack of or loss of humility.*—Samson is a clear example of how pride takes the place of humility and leads to destruction. Ananias and Sapphira in the Book of Acts afford an example of destruction due to a pretense of submission and humility. There are many today whose ministries, lives, and opportunities have been destroyed

because of lack of or the loss of humility! What God desires is for us to humble ourselves! Oh, how God honors and blesses with victory the humble life!

How can we be humble and happy? First Corinthians 3:21-23 explains the uselessness of a believer becoming involved in a bragging match with people. The passage says there is no need for this because we have it all already! Just remember you can afford to be happily humble (kind, loving, polite, quiet, behaved, serving, trusting) because it's all yours anyway! So don't be impatient. God is on the throne. He will humble those who proudly exalt themselves, and He will exalt those who humble themselves! So, be humble and happy.

How to Humble Self

We come now asking a probing question. This is such a sensitive area because we are not seeking the appearance of humility but the reality of humility. Jesus gives us insight, and He clearly shows His desire that we "humble ourselves."

> And he spake this parable unto certain which trusted in themselves that they were righteous, and despised others: Two men went up into the temple to pray; the one a Pharisee, and the other a publican. The Pharisee stood and prayed thus with himself, God, I thank thee, that I am not as other men are, extortioners, unjust, adulterers, or even as this publican. I fast twice in the week, I give tithes of all that I possess. And the publican, standing afar off, would not lift up so much as his eyes unto heaven, but smote upon his breast, saying, God be merciful to me a sinner. I tell you, this man went down to his house justified rather than the other: for every one that exalteth himself shall be abased; and he that humbleth himself shall be exalted (Luke 18:9-14).

In verses 9-12 we view the proud. In verses 13 and 14 we see the humble. There seem to be several self-humbling steps.

The Stance of Humility

"[He stood] afar off." It is not *how* we stand (slumped shoulders, cowed, whipped-dog look) but *where* we stand if we are humbling ourselves. This man was "afar off" and not pushing, shoving, or running for the front or demanding his rightful place. A tough self-action that will aid us in humbling ourselves is revealed in Luke 14:7-11. It seems to me that Jesus was bringing Himself under this same sort of humbling action in John 8:50 and 54 and also in John 6:15. Paul, no doubt, was taking seriously the self-humbling action in 2 Corinthians 10:17-18. John the Baptist understood this willful step toward humility when he testified, "He must increase, but I must decrease" (John 3:30). It is a bold and tough step when we voluntarily go to the unnoticed place at the back of the line, in order to humble ourselves. Trust God, He will call us forward if He wants to. If He does not, that means He has a plan, and we're going to have a tremendous time at the back of the line!

Gayle Erwin in his book *Jesus Style* speaks directly to this point. "Least is a choice you make when you have such a high view of others that you want to do all you can to elevate them and your position happens, because of your efforts in their behalf, to end up least . . . and you really didn't notice."[7]

The Stare of Humility

". . . would not lift up so much as his eyes unto heaven." This is a dramatic flesh-and-blood illustration of deep humility. The man realized who God was and who he was and was expressing precisely that in the direction he gazed. Practically, the Pharisee was comparing himself to others (v. 9). Here the publican compared himself to none other but saw himself in the presence of Almighty God. How does a humble person look? The humble person looks as if Jesus is the most important person in the world and that he is surrendered to Him.

Let me pause to make this urgent point. How are self-worth and self-esteem reconciled with self-humility? In my opinion, self-worth outside of the lordship of Christ is worthless. Never will believers be worth more or elevated higher than when they humble themselves at the feet of Jesus. So called self-worth and self-esteem outside of self-humility before Christ may bring great profits here, but it will leave you bankrupt hereafter.

The Smoting of Humility

". . . smote upon his breast." This is not some sort of self-flagellation but the expression of deep brokenness.

The Speech of Humility

". . . saying, God be merciful to me a sinner." Paul was saying the same in Romans 7:18, and the prodigal son confessed, "I have sinned" (Luke 15:21). How does humility sound? Humility sounds like a container or a channel which realizes that, if it were not for the One within, there would be no praise. Humility says, "Look inside of me, see who is coming through my life. It is not me, it is He!" (A good example of this is found in 1 Cor. 2:1-5).

These are some steps toward humbling ourselves: Stance, Stare, Smoting, Speech. But we must remember we are not seeking the *appearance* of humility but the *reality* of humility. Someone might say now, "I don't think I'm going to like this humbling of myself." Of course, you won't! The old nature will hate it! But God will love it, honor it, and bless it! Jesus will help us accomplish it, and we'll find it not only the reflection of Christ but such a relaxation to the alternative. "Take my yoke upon you, and learn of me; for I am *meek* and *lowly* in heart: and ye shall find rest unto your souls" (Matt. 11:29, author's italics).

20 | A SIMPLIFIED LIFE

No man that warreth entangleth himself with the affairs of this life; that he may please him who hath chosen him to be a soldier (2 Tim. 2:4).

"Brethren, I count not myself to have apprehended: but this one thing I do, forgetting those things which are behind, . . . I press toward the mark for the prize of the high calling of God in Christ Jesus. Let us therefore, as many as be perfect, be thus minded: and if in anything ye be otherwise minded, God shall reveal even this unto you" (Phil. 3:13-15).

A servant will never have the flexibility to respond and intercede if his life is not one of simplicity. *The aim of a simplified life is to free us to be more of a servant and intercessor. A simplified life touches our schedules, commitments, possessions, activities, money, talents, and such. We may expect of the simplified life freedom, joy, and usefulness.*

The first step toward a simplified life is a simplified commitment to the Lord. You cannot serve two masters at the same time. "This one thing I do" declares that I have decided to enter into the joys and the rewards of a servant/intercessor life.

Hebrews 12:1-2 is a transparent picture of a life committed to following the life-style of Jesus with our eyes fixed on eternity. The "game plan" and strategy of such a servant life is clear. "Lay aside every weight and the sin which doth so easily beset us" (v.1) is an expression of a simplified life. The runner strips away everything that will hinder him.

147

In Vietnam my small scout platoon was often isolated from friendly troops and had to have considerable speed and flexibility in order to survive. Consequently we left all nonessentials behind. The slogan, "Travel light, freeze at night, stay all right." There were some inconveniences that went with this simplified life philosophy. For example, we ate less, we often slept cold and wet, we missed hot meals and some other creature comforts. However, it was worth it to stay alive!

When Captain Eddie Rickenbacker and his companions of the ill-fated World War II air expedition in the South Seas prepared to abandon their plane, they threw out everything that was movable. "In the face of death," Rickenbacker said, "if you ever think that material things are worth anything, ladies and gentlemen, have that experience, and you will find out how useless they are, no matter how you may have cherished them."

It is worth the so-called inconveniences of a simplified life in order to be alert spiritually and to serve and intercede! Dear Christian, are you truly active in Christ? Someone might commend me for being wise to adopt such a philosophy during war. But it was not my wisdom, I was only doing what I had been taught and trained to do. *We believers have been taught and trained how to survive in spiritual warfare and if you will look at the manual (the Bible) closely and the life of Christ, you will find that a simplified life is essential for spiritual survival.*

May I offer some considerations for the simplified life?

1. *Freedom from fear.* — leads to a simplified life which in turn shows itself in a bold stand and witness as a servant/intercessor. We will take a bolder witness and stand because our simplified life has left us so little to lose! Hallelujah! Many of us have so clogged, confused, and complicated our lives, with things and places, that we cannot even stand, let alone go as Jesus desires and commands us to do. We resemble David in Saul's armor! "David . . . tried whether he had strength to walk in this unwanted array and said, 'I cannot freely move in these' " (1 Sam. 17:39, Knox and Moffatt).What do I do? Do I sell all, give all

away, live like a hermit, become antisocial? *No one but the Holy Spirit can tell you what you personally will have to do to simplify your life. It is a treacherous thing to advise another on this subject or to listen to advice from others. All that is said or heard on this subject must be filtered through the Word of God, the life of Christ, and the ministry of the Holy Spirit. To do otherwise may cause you to make sincere but miserable mistakes.* You can trust the Lord to lead you once you become earnest on this matter.

2. *Distributors, not collectors, will be our calling in the simplified life.*—"Sticky-fingered" Christians that feel like they must have and hang onto something will find it very difficult to simplify their lives. To be sure, God may permit us to have things, but our desire will be to use and *distribute* those things, not merely to collect them.

3. *Do not question other servant life-styles.*—This includes even your mate and your children. Most find they become preoccupied with searching themselves about the servant life, and don't have time to question others.

4. *Refuse the call of this consumption-oriented Western world.*—A simplified life will demand great care when exposed to TV, magazines, catalogs, malls, and the like.

5. *Examine your life-style continually.*—What you do, what you spend, and what you involve yourself in should all be sifted by the question, "Am I doing this because of social guilt, status, pressure, or to be my Savior's servant and intercessor?" We should never order our lives by what others are doing or by what we want to do. A servant has a higher calling.

6. *Start somewhere.*—It is not an easy task to simplify your life. It has some similarities to cleaning out a closet or the garage. If you fondle a possession too long in trying to make up your mind about whether it stays or goes, you'll likely keep it. Something must go if your life is going to become simpler. Do not be surprised if you have painful trouble over the smallest item. It may take some time before you realize a significantly simplified life.

Know this—This simplifying of life is the very point where you will find out just how deeply infected you have become by the world and its philosophy of materialism.

There is a perceptive truth that attended the people of God who were reduced to the most simplified life in the wilderness as He provided them manna day by day. The truth is "He that gathered much had nothing over, and he that gathered little had no lack" (Ex. 16:18). It seems clear that God has a plan to show Himself through the simplified life. We must come to the place where we desire less, need less, and use less so we can go more and give more for Christ's sake. There is no other way to achieve this than the simplified life!

21 | HOLY GROUND

As I began to come to grips with the deep meaning of self-denial, sacrifice, and suffering in relationship to the believer there seemed to be a sure word to me from the Lord. I was well aware these were areas in which I had almost no experience for His sake or the gospel's sake. He seemed to say what I so sincerely felt, "You are now beginning to walk on holy ground."

I found myself reading Acts 7:31-34 over again, as well as the related passage of Exodus 3:4-6. I thought of the willing self-denial, sacrifice, and suffering of Abraham, Isaac, Jacob, and of "thy fathers" in the faith, including those of recent years. Before me came the scenes of those hundreds burned at the stake, the thousands devoured in Rome, and the hundreds of thousands who have died for their faith in recent years. Further, there are those tens of thousands of unforgettables who rotted away, unnamed and unnoticed, in Communist prison cells, and their mates and their children. Even today, prisons and labor camps are full of faithful believers who have committed no crime except to love Jesus. These take into no account the dedicated Christians around the world that are harassed, discriminated against, denied jobs, education, and housing all because of their faith. Most of them go for a lifetime unnamed and unnoticed. As I thought of many American Christians, but most especially of myself, and self-denial, sacrifice, and suffering for Jesus and the gospel's sake, my eyes fogged and my lips whispered, "Yes, Lord, *holy* ground." Not only had I failed to walk upon this holy ground, but I was certain I had no right even to speak of such, certainly not to teach about such a subject.

Then the Lord spoke to my heart, "You may teach from the pulpit what I'm trying to teach you about self-denial, sacrifice, and suffering, but only under one condition. You must do it without shoes on your feet, 'Put off thy shoes from thy feet, for the place whereon thou standest is holy ground'" (Ex. 3:5).

Needless to say, my heart was bombarded by multiplied reasons not to do such an uncharacteristic and odd thing. This would surely go on for week after week, for months.

Happily, I had about six months before reaching these subjects in my teaching and prayed in order to know for sure this was His will. It was, and I explained the above to the Sunday morning congregation.

Carefully pointing out that this was no attendance-getting gimmick, and that I would not be interested in any joking, I gave them my heartfelt reasons for putting off my shoes.

1 To *obey* the Lord.
2. To *confess* my lack of experience in these areas. (My bare feet were to be a reminder that I was confessing.)
3. To *honor* those who have given us such testimony of God's glorious grace through their self-denial, sacrifice, and suffering for Christ and the gospel's sake.

My intentions were not to speak anymore from the pulpit about why I wore no shoes, and whatever explanation might be needed, the congregation could give it. Additionally, I made it clear that I hoped this would not make anyone ill at ease or embarrass them. However, my main concern was not to embarrass myself before the Lord by being disobedient.

As I explained this, it was apparent by the attention, silence, and some low tones—and a few moderate shouts—that the people had also heard the Spirit in this matter.

There were several touching acts that occurred during that service as I began this study on self-denial, sacrifice, and suffering. Several said they pulled their shoes off, too, some literally—

others in their heart. Later the soloist said he wanted to pull his shoes off to sing but felt the Lord said, "wait." At the invitation many came to the altar, among whom were two older teenage boys feeling the call to preach. Before we stopped praying they arose from their knees to return to their seats. As they did I felt their hands pat my shoeless feet. They understood. With deep humility we were now moving onto "holy ground." May the truths of these next pages become holy ground for your life as well.

22 | SELF-DENIAL

He must increase, but I must decrease (John 3:30).

We have been studying in some length and detail the servant life which is found to be the life of an intercessor—one who intervenes and intercedes as a response to the Person of Jesus living in them.

Such a life is absolutely vital because the servant/intercessor is in the life of Christ to whom we are to be conformed. And the believer's station of coreigning and coruling throughout eternity is based upon this life (Matt. 20:26). So there is a glorious level of living, both broad and blessed, called servant/intercessor. To the unspiritual eye this place seems low and despicable but, in truth, it is a holy place that gives unspeakable joy regardless of circumstances. But for a believer to live at this level of submission for any length of time and to have much impact with intercession, the believer must understand and grasp three more Bible truths that are interwoven and interrelated to the servant/intercessor life. These are: *Self-denial, Sacrifice,* and *Suffering.* We are now involving ourselves in spiritual "excavation." We are looking beneath the surface of the servant life to see what it is built upon, level by level.

As we consider what the Bible teaches about these truths they seem like a table with three legs. The surface, which is broad and most noticeable, is that of the servant/intercessor ministry, but what substantiates its usefulness are the three legs of self-denial, sacrifice, and suffering. These truths also relate to one another

154

like the interconnecting sleeves of a telescope—each extending out of the other. However, to me, the clearest way to understand the relationship of these three to the servant life is to see them as three doors inside the servants' quarters. Experientially we will find that if we live in the servants' quarters there will be these three doorways (self-denial, sacrifice, and suffering), and the servant/intercessor will find himself continually and inescapably circulating through these passageways. By the way, the thresholds of the three doorways have been worn smooth by countless thousands who have also followed Jesus in the sacrificial life. The servant/intercessor will find that these truths do, in fact, build one upon the other like building blocks.

To serve and help others means to turn away from self-interests. The essence and core of self-denial is sacrifice. If you deny self for Christ's sake as a servant/intercessor you will without fail experience sacrifice. Likewise "sacrifice" implies and builds upon suffering. The Bible demonstrates this truth in many ways from the sacrificial lamb in the Old Testament to the sacrificial Lamb of the New Testament. A worthy sacrifice will require some suffering. Do not expect that this truth will change in connection with us as the Christian servant/intercessor. Therefore underneath the servant life is self-denial, underneath self-denial is sacrifice, and underneath sacrifice is suffering. All of these truths are *inescapably* interrelated and interwoven. I do not know of any biblical exception to this. Certainly this is the way of Christ's life. We must agree it does, on the surface, appear to be "The Sacrificed Life."

Self-denial

"He must increase, but I must decrease" is the most concise and clear statement on the truth and depth of a life of self-denial for the believer. The life of the believer is exactly like the sand of an hourglass which is either on one side or the other (Matt. 6:24). If Christ's presence increases, then self's presence *must* decrease. If self's presence increases, then Christ's present will decrease. We speak not of losing Christ but of His lack of manifestation through us due to our self-life. This is a most personal thing, "*I* must decrease"—*self*-denial.

There are other texts which add volume and life to this inescapable truth (Mark 8:31-38; Luke 5:11; Matt. 19:27-30; Luke 14:33). "So likewise, whosoever he be of you that forsaketh not all that he hath, he cannot be my disciple" (Luke 14:33). Do you hear the force and lack of reservation—"all"? We have been saved to give up "all!" This sounds like a death warrant. It cuts to the bone and makes us cry out, "How can this be?" "It can't be!" Ah, but it is true! Please do not attempt to spiritualize this literal truth away in order to save yourself on earth, only to suffer loss hereafter. The truth is that this is not a death warrant at all, but rather a spiritual life announcement! "And he that taketh not his cross, and followeth after me is not worthy of me. He that findeth his life shall lose it: and he that loseth his life for my sake shall find it" (Matt. 10:38-39).

Missionary Jim Elliot, who died at the hands of the Aucas to whom he gave himself as a servant/intercessor in the jungles of Ecuador, uttered these unforgettable words, "He is no fool that gives what he cannot keep to gain what he cannot lose." Thus the parting word of a grain of wheat as it falls into the ground is, "He must increase, but I must decrease." Can we accept it? Will we live it?

Self-denial is both the *spirit* and *action* of John 3:30. God expects believers to have both. We are to have the spirit—attitude of self-denial, as well as the actions literally to deny self. While God *expects* both attitude and action He does not always *require* both. Abraham and Isaac demonstrate that God does not always desire the blood of denial but that He tests us to determine our spirit and attitude of self-denial. Be careful never to pretend about having the spirit and attitude of self-denial unless you are prepared to back it up with the action of self-denial (remember Ananias and Sapphira, Acts 5).

Self-denial is the expected result of putting Christ first in everything, every way, on every day. If anything but the love of Christ brings on self-denial it is of no value in eternity. We are not called to self-denial to purify our bodies or to escape this world. We simply find ourselves being denied because we have allowed Christ to have His way through us to serve and intercede with and for those for whom He died. Yes, it is Christ increasing and us decreasing! As self is denied we find ourselves less encumbered and more able to quickly and wholeheartedly follow Him. Self-denial is the way—the spirit and action—of Christ's life. Jesus would give anything and do anything, stop anywhere, go anywhere—even to the extent of dying. His was and is a life of self-denial. Now Jesus can live by the same attitude and action of self-denial within you and me if we allow Him to have His way through us.

Self-denial says, "You must always remember that Calvary comes *before Pentecost.*" There is no shortcut to salvation and to consecration. Self-denial is a tangible expression of the fact that nothing is more valuable to us than Christ's way through us as servant/intercessors for souls.

A. J. Gordon gives us an example of this from nature. He said, "Two saplings grew up side by side. Through the action of the wind they crossed each other. By and by each became wounded by the friction. The sap began to mingle until one calm day they became attached. Then the stronger began to absorb the weaker. It became larger and larger while the other withered and declined until it finally dropped away and disappeared. And now there are two trunks at the bottom and only one at the top. Death has taken away one; life has triumphed in the other."

Such is the blessed way of His increase and our decrease! May I remind us that the shade, the beauty, the strength, and the fruit of those two trees that became one are but a glimpse of the positive, productive, and joyful way of life for the servant/intercessor who follows Jesus through the door of self-denial.

> Though I am crucified with Thee
> and bear the marks of Calvary,
> yet still I live and gladly cry,
> 'tis Thou in me, not I, not I.
>
> —Anonymous[8]

Why Self-denial?

Again, self-denial is what happens to self when we put Christ first. Why teach self-denial today? Are we getting prepared to die in some prison cell or by a firing squad for our faith? No, I do not believe that the average Western-world congregation is in any great threat of a martyr's massacre.

However, I want to be quick to emphasize that it is entirely likely that there is a generation listening and reading today that may face such an end, and it also may be that there are several who are now sharing these truths who will one day be called upon to give their lives in Christ's service somewhere. (If this is correct, "Dear Lord Jesus, may these truths be caught!") Most of us will not fall into either category. Nonetheless, the truth of the servant's self-denial is just as relevant in the free world as in a foreign concentration camp.

But why self-denial? To that question there are two answers both contained in one fact about Christ's death. That fact is, *Jesus did not die for Himself!* Jesus died for two selfless reasons:

1. For the Father—"Thy will be done" (Matt. 6:10).
2. For others—"Came not to be ministered unto, but . . . to give his life a ransom for many" (Matt. 20:28).

Christ's two selfless reasons should be our same two selfless reasons for denying ourselves. We are to deny ourselves for the Father because His plan is to work through the servant/intercessor's life. We are to deny ourselves for others as is stated in 1 John 3:16, "Hereby perceive we the love of God, because he laid down his life for us: and we ought to lay down our lives for the brethren." How did we know of the love of God? Jesus denied Himself and died. How will others know the love of God? We will deny ourselves as Christ intercedes through us. Verses 17-19 give a clarifying example. There are also other texts about our denying ourselves that others may see the love of God (Rom. 12:10-14; 2 Cor. 4:5; 5:14-15; Gal. 5:13; 1 Thess. 2:7-8; Heb. 10:24).

So we see that self-denial is essential for the depth of servant/ intercessor living. Again, we see self-denial is a positive, productive, joyful way of life!

Earlier I cautioned us all that the flesh will want to draw back from "The Sacrificed Life." At the point of self-denial is where you may say, "Here's where I get off!" Frankly, this is precisely where most of us prepare to disassociate ourselves from Jesus' way. I squirm and sweat under the implications of self-denial, sacrifice, and suffering. I think of those who urge Jesus to leave them alone (Mark 5:17). Then the Lord reminds me of Philippians 3:15, that He would make us aware should we start to follow after anything but Himself. Also, Hebrews 10:38 says that we are not to be numbered among those in whom He has no pleasure because they did draw back. "For it had been better for them not to have known the way of righteousness, than, after they have known it, to turn from the holy commandment delivered unto them. But it is happened unto them according to the true proverb, The dog is turned to his own vomit again; and the sow that was washed to her wallowing in the mire" (2 Pet. 2:21-22). It is also impossible for me to explain away Luke 14:27-28, "And whosoever doth not bear his cross, and come after me, cannot be my disciple. For which of you, intending to build a tower, sitteth not down first, and counteth the cost, whether he have sufficient to finish it?"

At such a point of hesitation we must remember the promise of the cross: "The greater the brokenness, the greater the blessing." Then as that same Jesus rises up in us, to be Himself, we hear our own lips repeat, "Father, . . . nevertheless not as I will, but as thou wilt" (Matt. 26:39).

But where is this route of servant/intercessor and self-denial to go? Where are the areas of life that the Bible and Christ teach us that we are to be prepared to deny self? About a dozen of these areas seem apparent, most of which I have drawn together from my own study under three headings: 1. Excesses, 2. Exaltations, 3. Essentials.

Self-denial of Excesses

He went away sorrowful: for he had great possessions (Matt.
19:22).

Excess means extras, comforts, abundance, luxuries, plenty—
"the exceedingly abundant." Matthew 6:19-21 speaks of storing
up. What do we store up? We store up the plenty, the extras, the
abundance, the excess. Jesus is saying here that we're not to
concentrate on keeping the excess of the world for ourselves, but
we are to concentrate on what will count throughout eternity.

The account of the rich young ruler has many lessons (Matt.
19:16-22). There is little doubt that among these lessons one factor is for sure: Jesus is trying, searching, and testing this person at
the point of his riches, plenty, abundance, and excess—"for he
had great possessions." What was needed for this man to be
pleasing and acceptable in the sight of Jesus? It was not that he
was to become poverty-stricken. It was not that he should care
for all the poor in the world. No, what would have made this
pleasing and acceptable in the sight of Christ was for him to obey
the Lord, deny self of his riches, and follow Christ. This man was
a miserable failure because he would not deny self of the excess.
Consequently, he went away sorrowfully.

The big question is, Are we willing and prepared to deny self
when it comes to our excess, abundance, and plenty? We have
no need to concern ourselves with what excesses we are to deny
ourselves, because the Holy Spirit will deal with us at whatever
point He chooses—and we will know it when He does. Further,
it is not our business to look at another believer's excess and make
a judgment as to their spirit and action of self-denial. If we take
seriously self-denial of our excesses, we may be sure we will hear
a self-centered voice somewhere along the line say, "You sure are
giving up a lot!" But remember the voice of the Lord Jesus that
says in the lesson about the unfaithful servant, "Unto whomsoever much is given, of him shall be much required" (Luke
12:48).

Someone has said to the effect, "A standard of luxury living is the god of the twentieth-century Western world, and the advertising man is its prophet and preacher." We of the church may not bend our knees to such a god, but it appears that we are prone to bow our heads in its presence. Only by God's grace and intense personal effort can we escape the soft cushion of luxury that has almost smothered Christian compassion out of us and robbed us of the eternal joy of the servant/intercessor life.

Billy Graham is credited with saying, "The American Christian church has traded its cross for a cushion." Some of us started "hot and hard" but now most of our Christian life has become cool, soft, and slow. There were days when it cost us something to live for the Lord—now it seems that mostly it pays well. (Have you ever noticed that the few testimonies you do hear of self-denial usually come from the person's distant past?) Even our churches, for the most part, are not places where we deny self to do a divine duty but often are places where we come to a cafeteria of comforts and conveniences. Church is a soft, easy, comfortable, luxurious experience. If it is not such an experience then the attendee can always go to the "other caviar cathedral" up the road or stay home and watch four at one time from Korea to Kalamazoo via satellite on a supersized screen with absolutely no stress or strain upon their excesses, extras, comforts, abundance, luxury, and plenty.

Let us face it. Such is not the road that Jesus traveled! On Jesus' brow was a crown, not of gold but of thorns. His hands and feet were not jeweled with diamonds but pierced with spikes. His body was not draped with silk but dripping with blood for lost and sin-afflicted mankind. We may be assured that if we step upon the treadmill of the servant/intercessor life our flabby faith of ease and excess will be tested at the point of self-denial. We must remember that what the hordes of hellcats could not do to Samson in open and fierce confrontation the soft stroking of creature comfort and sensual pleasure did in the lap of Delilah. What atheistic Communism and Satan cannot do in open confrontation is being done today as the "Christian" Western world lays its head (and spiritual neck) in the lap of luxury and excess and refuses to give any of it up for the sake of Christ. While it may seem our Lord has entrusted the church of America with the money bag, we must be on guard lest our selfishness betray Christ as Judas did.

I shall never forget the eyewitness report of starving Christians in prison with bleeding ankles and wrists from chains who knelt in rags upon a wet, stinking dungeon floor and prayed that the Christians in the Western world would not be so overcome by their plenty of comfort that they would fail to respond to the cries of a lost and dying world. Can we bear the thought of prayers from those who have denied themselves unto prison, chains, starvation, and even death that comforts would not separate *us here* from Christ's call upon our life?

Doesn't that drive us to our knees? Don't we want to cry out, "Lord, I am your servant and intercessor. Search me, test me, try me at my excess. Prepare me to deny myself of whatever excess that will please You to intercede for others"?

May God give us the spirit of Epaphras (Col. 1:7) who voluntarily shared Paul's prison in order to help as a "dear fellow servant." Such a spirit of self-denial will be required if we intercede.

Hudson Taylor of the China Inland Mission grasped the truth of self-denial in order to intercede as he was preparing for the mission field. Here is a quote from Taylor's diary.

Having now the twofold object in view of accustoming myself to endure hardness, and economizing in order to be able to more largely assist those among whom I spent a good deal of time laboring in the gospel, I soon found that I could live upon very much less than I had previously thought possible. Butter, milk, and other such luxuries I soon ceased to use; and I found that by living mainly on oatmeal and rice, with occasional variation, a very small sum was sufficient for my needs. In this way I had more than two-thirds of my income available for other purposes; and my experience was that the less I spent on myself and the more I gave away, the fuller of happiness and blessing did my soul become. Unspeakable joy all the day long, and everyday, was my happy experience. God, even my God, was a living, bright reality; and all I had to do was joyfully serve.[9]

Should not the standard of living for the servant/intercessor be one of less desire, less use, less waste, resulting in more with which to intercede. Such a standard of living is demonstrated clearly in the life of Christ and many great saints of God through the ages, as well as the Scriptures. Such a life for the believer is not easy because, as Hudson Taylor put it on another occasion, "It is possible to say, 'My all is on the altar,' and yet be unprepared to sacrifice a ring from one's finger, or a picture from one's wall, or a child from one's family, for the salvation of the heathen." To fail to deny self of excess, comfort, luxuries, abundance, and plenty in order to intercede as a servant is but to, in the words of John Wesley, "demonstrate that we are living men but dead Christians."

It is obvious that Christ has come that we might have life and have it more abundantly. "Life" more abundantly, not things.

Self-denial of Exaltations

Self-exaltation is the aspect of our lives that is in direct opposition to humility. Humility is essential for the servant/intercessor life. I have dealt a bit with self-exaltation under the heading of "Humility," but it is at the point of self-denial that we must really come to grips with the exaltation of oneself.

Self is a most selfish and subtle enemy, and we must be prepared to deny self in some of the most painful places: our talents, our intellect, our skills, our abilities, and sometimes even our spiritual gifts. Failure to acknowledge self-exaltation at these points is certain to doom the servant/intercessor's effectiveness because self-exaltation will rob us of God's power in these areas. We usually see our abilities, talents, skills, etc., as Watchman Nee said, "Harmless and very profitable for the kingdom's service." It is true that they can be just that, provided we have denied self of any exaltation because of them and place these under Christ. To allow self to be exalted in these areas will cause them to be utterly useless to the kingdom's service. We are dealing with a critical but often unobserved truth, even to those who are otherwise spiritual people. Children must be taught this truth. Youth must be reminded of this truth. Adults must never forget this truth. All must constantly deny self of personal exaltation in order that we may decrease and He increase.

First Thessalonians 1:5 tells us that the gospel did not come "in word only, but also in power." Paul speaks directly to this emphasis in 2 Corinthians 4:5, "For we preach not ourselves, but Christ Jesus the Lord; and ourselves your servants for Jesus' sake." This is further expanded in Philippians 3:4-8 and in 1 Corinthians 2:1-5.

The point is: natural abilities, talents, skills, and the like cannot impart spiritual life to us or anyone else. There must be the power of God. First Corinthians 15:48 tells us that which is of the earth is "earthy" and that which is of heaven is "heavenly." John 6:44 says, "No man can come to me, except the Father which hath sent me draw him." It must be understood that spiritual gifts selfishly used fall into the same useless category as talents and abilities without the power of God.

Therefore we must inwardly and outwardly deny self of exaltation coming to us as a result of our talents, abilities, skills, and intellect. We are not to trust in these things alone. We are to keep them under Christ and see self as helpless. When I go to my knees just before preaching I usually quote Zechariah 4:6 to myself and before the Lord, "Not by might, nor by power, but by my spirit, saith the Lord of hosts." As I adjust my tie or coat before leaving to minister and intercede, the Spirit seems always to ask me, "Have you appropriately groomed yourself spiritually for power?" What good is anything and everything if there is no power from on high? Samson forever reminds us of the folly of being without the power, "And he wist not that the Lord was departed from him" (Judg. 16:20).

How Do We Deny Self of This Personal Exaltation?

1. *Thank* the Lord for our talents, intellects, skills, abilities, and so forth. Place them under the Lord.

2. *Confess* that even with these things, "Lord, I am helpless!"
3. *Direct* all praise and exaltation away from ourselves and to the Lord. (This can be done sweetly and unpharisaically. Otherwise, we will come across as having spiritual pride and arrogance.) This is not an appeal for "syrupy and false humility" but for "sanctified common sense."

There are some honest questions that accompany these considerations.

Question: "Aren't these God-given abilities for His use?"

Answer: "Yes, but are we using them for ourselves or Him or for both ourselves and him?" If self enters into it then these things become of no account because God is not going to share His glory. If a football player talks about his "God-given ability" and at the same time testifies of Christ in his life, that is a wonderful thing. But if he does this to portray himself as macho or to gain favor of some girl or her parents, then it is all useless.

Question: "Well then, isn't it better to be a secret and silent saint and not risk self-exaltation?"

Answer: "No, for this too will rob the blessing of God's power." If Satan cannot foul you up he will try to shut you up. Usually Satan fouls us up to shut us up. We are not to be silent, but we are to do what causes Christ to increase and gives glory to God!

Question: "What about those things that are obviously of the flesh but give off the appearance of being successfully blessed of God?"

Answer: "Such misconceptions usually stem from our distorted standard of success, numbers, TV shows, radio programs, books, etc." These are not necessarily marks of being "successfully blessed of God." But we must admit that sometimes limited but lasting results do come out of such situations. Such an exception can be explained by the prayers, life, and efforts of other self-denying and godly people involved in such ministries and endeavors. We should never forget that the Bible, regardless of how it is made known, will not return void.

But do not lose sight of this. Our concern is not with the "what ifs" or "what abouts." Our concern is that Christ increase and we decrease in all areas of our servant/intercessory ministry.

The acid test is not whether we use our abilities, talents, and skills in a moving and smooth way, or if they receive a positive response by people wanting more of them. Nor is the test whether or not these gifts cause people to do as we ask or suggest. The acid test is after people have been exposed to our abilities, gifts, talents, skills, do they take on spiritual life and become more like Christ? (We are aware that *most* did not respond in such a way even to Christ's presence. However, we cannot forget that many did!) We must be honest. Is our life expressed through talents, intellects, skills, abilities, and even spiritual gifts only gathering earthly plaques, applause, compliments, crowns, promotions, or awards (which are made of wood, hay, and stubble and shall be burned and never allowed to enter eternity)? Or do these areas of expression increase Christ and, therefore, impart spiritual life by His power?

Let us note two dangerous mistakes that will rob the servant intercessor's ministry of God's blessing and power.

1. *We should never think that God will not call upon us to minister from weakness.*—In fact, weakness is the place where most sense their great helplessness and their need for heaven's help. First Corinthians 2:3 says, "And I was with you in much weakness." First Corinthians 15:43 says that the body is, "sown in weakness; . . . raised in power." Hebrews 11:34 says of the faithful that, "Out of weakness were made strong." Jesus' words in 2 Corinthians 12:9 are, "My grace is sufficient for thee: for my strength is made perfect in weakness." Paul continues following the words of Christ and says, "Most gladly therefore will I rather glory in my infirmities, that the power of Christ may rest upon me." Weakness is a wonderful thing in the servant/intercessor's life if it has been brought under Christ. Some of the most meaningful solos ever sung have been those where the singer forgot the words but through their weakness and failure, out of God's grace, went on that Christ might increase whether or not they were exalted. Usually every sweeping and lasting revival begins

with a believer's confession of weakness and helplessness. This, then, is the essence of 1 Corinthians 1:26-31.

2. *Never think that you are only to minister in the areas of your spiritual gifts.*—God has not given the believer spiritual gifts in order that he may become a "spiritual specialist" by refusing to minister outside his gifts. In a dark, unfamiliar room sometimes a hand acts and ministers like an eye. The whole body benefits and rejoices when it is discovered that without such action it would have fallen down three flights of stairs! So we are to be careful at our strengths and we are to be willing at our weaknesses.

May I suggest making two lists. One list will comprise your abilities, skills, talents, intellect, and spiritual gifts. List everything from jogging one-half mile to quoting a verse of Scripture to saw-ing a board straight or displaying mercy and compassion. Then *thank* Him for these things and *confess*, "Lord, I am helpless even with these things." *Direct* praise to Him for these things and their possibilities in the kingdom's service.

The second list should be comprised of our weaknesses, fears, and failures, not sins. List them all. Then *thank* Him that he is able to use even our weaknesses for His glory! *Confess* your helplessness without His help. *Direct* praise to Him even before He uses these things and especially after you see His miracle work through your weakness!

How easy it is to selfishly shun our weaknesses and thereby rob God's power and miss God's blessing. How easy it is to shine selfishly in our strength and also rob God's power and miss God's blessing. But how essential it is for the servant/intercessor to deny self and lay both strengths and weaknesses at Christ's feet and allow His power to show through our helpless nothingness.

I carry a little card that has these words written upon it. "The peak of servant life is never to ask anything for yourself, never refuse a cross for Christ, and always accept life humbly as it comes without questions as the allowed will of God." For a servant/intercessor is not one who possesses great light from God but one who possesses nothing! Through this nothing shines God's power to endure the worst, to love the worst, to hope in the worst for the best through Christ, and see Christ increase and me decrease.

Richard Wurmbrand relates a true story based upon Luke 22:33-34 and 62.

> A sword was put to the chest of a Christian and he was asked, "Are you a Christian?" When he answered, "Yes," they were ready to kill him, but an officer said, "Free him, he is an idiot." Someone asked the man later, "How could you confess Christ with such courage?" And his reply was, "I read the story of Peter's denial of Christ, and I did not wish to weep bitterly."[10]

Whether it is self-denial at the point of excess, exaltation, essentials, family, and/or life, it is far better to deny self here than to "weep bitterly" hereafter because we denied Christ instead of self.

Self-denial of Essentials

> And Jesus said unto him, Foxes have holes, and birds of the air have nests; but the Son of man hath not where to lay his head. (Luke 9:58).

After hearing what Jesus spoke about Himself we then see what Jesus said about His disciples.

> Go your ways: behold, I send you forth as lambs among wolves. Carry neither purse, nor scrip, nor shoes: and salute no man by the way. And into whatsoever house ye enter, first say, Peace be to this house. And if the son of peace be there, your peace shall rest upon it: if not, it shall turn to you again. And in the same house remain, eating and drinking such things as they give: for the laborer is worthy of his hire. Go not from house to house (Luke 10:3-7).

The declaration that brings with it denial in Matthew 6:24-34 says that we are to be preoccupied with the kingdom (the reign and rule of God) in our lives. Question: "Would we ever be required to give up essentials/necessities, shelter, food, drink?"

To most of us "essentials" mean those things we feel that we *must* have. However, this is a relative term. For instance, Hudson

Taylor felt that milk and butter were luxuries and bread and oat-meal were necessities. Most of us of the Western world feel like three square meals a day are essentials. Someone has observed that most Westerners honestly think they barely have enough to survive on in modest comfort. The truth is that we have allowed the advertising man to rename luxuries—calling them necessities. Five hundred million men, women, and children in the world on this very day are starving, making a total of at least one billion in extreme hunger.

What so-called "necessities" would most of us in the Western world have to give up to be where the remainder of the world is? Economist Robert Heilbroner has itemized the abandoned "luxuries." We begin by invading the house of our imaginary Western family to *strip it* of its furniture. *Everything goes*: beds, chairs, tables, television set, lamps. We will leave the family with a few old blankets, a kitchen table, a wooden chair. Along with the bureaus go the *clothes*. Each member of the family may keep in his "wardrobe" his oldest suit or dress, a shirt or blouse. We will permit *a pair of shoes* for the *head of the family*, but none for the wife or children.

We move to the kitchen. The appliances have already been taken out, so we turn to the cupboards. The box of matches may stay, a small bag of flour, some sugar, and salt. A few moldy potatoes, already in the rubbish bin, must be hastily rescued, for they will provide much of tonight's meal. We will leave a handful of onions and a dish of dried beans. All the rest we take away: the meat, the fresh vegetables, the canned goods.

Now we have stripped the house: the bathroom has been dismantled, the running water shut off, the electric wires taken out. Next we take away the house. The family can move to the tool-shed.

Communications must go next. No more newspapers, magazines, books—not that they are missed, since we must take away our family's literacy as well. Instead, *in our shantytown we will allow one radio.*

Now government services must go. No more postman, no

more firemen. There is a school, but it is three miles away and consists of two classrooms. There are, of course, no hospitals or doctors nearby. The nearest clinic is ten miles away and is tended by a midwife. It can be reached by bicycle, provided that the family has a bicycle, which is unlikely.

Finally, money. We will allow our family a cash hoard of about $5.00. This will prevent our breadwinner from experiencing the tragedy of a peasant who went blind because he could not raise the $3.94 which he mistakenly thought he needed to receive admission to a hospital where he could have been cured.[11]

How many of our Christian brothers and sisters confront this kind of grinding poverty today?

In R. J. Sider's book, *Rich Christians in the Age of Hunger*, he tells that the tears and agony of all such people mentioned above who are down to the real bare-bones necessities can be summed up in the following situation. The Alarin family of seven live in an 8′ × 10′ room. Cooking utensils are their only furniture. Mr. Alarin makes eighty cents on good days as an ice vendor. Several times a month, Mrs. Alarin stays up all night to make a coconut sweet which she sells on the street. Total income for the midnight toil: fifty cents. The family had not tasted meat for a month when Stan Mooneyham of World Vision visited Mrs. Alarin recently: Tears washed her dark, sunken eye sockets as she spoke: "I feel so sad when my children cry at night because they have no food. I know my life will never change. What can I do to solve my problems? I am so worried about the future of my children. I want them to go to school but how can we afford it? I am sick most of the time, but I can't go to the doctor because each visit costs thirty cents and the medicine is extra. What can I do?" She broke down into quiet sobbing. I admit without shame that I wept with her. World poverty is a hundred million mothers weeping, like Mrs. Alarin, because they cannot feed their children.[12]

We must be careful at this point. It will be easy to say that such people as these are "not trying," "they could do better," or, "Well, it's their own fault." For most of these people this would simply not be true because they have been caught in circumstances they cannot alter. Why these people are in these situations is beside the point that I am trying to make. My point is: if so many of the world live on so little, what then really are our own essentials and necessities? Whatever you and I decide are our real necessities, we need to be prepared and willing to deny these things should the servant/intercessor life require it.

Are there any Bible cases that talk about denying oneself of necessities? Giving out of poverty is clearly seen in 2 Corinthians 8:1-5. Once you read that passage of Scripture several lessons seem to leap out. In spite of trial, affliction, and poverty these believers gave happily. They gave immediately without waiting until they had more. They gave more than they could "comfortably afford." They went beyond the limits that the community would have expected of them. No one had to beg or coerce them. They insisted on giving. They realized that poverty (below necessities) was no excuse. Nor could prayer be a substitute for tangible intercession as they were given opportunity and led by the Spirit. The secret of denying self of necessities is found in verse 5. "And this they did, not as we hoped, but first gave their own selves to the Lord, and unto us by the will of God." They had surrendered themselves so they could make a happy surrender of their substance.

A businessman and a lawyer, both Christians, were traveling in Korea. One day they saw in the fields by the side of the road a young man pulling a rude plow, while an old man held the handles. The lawyer was amused and took a snapshot of the scene. "That's a curious picture! I suppose they are very poor," he said to the missionary who was interpreter and guide to the party. "Yes," was the quiet reply. "That is the family of Chi Boui. When the church was being built they were eager to give something to it, but they had no money, so they sold their only ox and gave the money to the church. This spring they are pulling the plow themselves." The lawyer and the businessman by his side were silent for some moments. Then the businessman said, "That must have been a real sacrifice."

"They did not call it that," said the missionary. "They thought it was fortunate that they had the ox to sell." The lawyer and the businessman did not have much more to say. When they reached home the lawyer took the picture to his minister and told him about it. "I want to double my pledge to the church," he said. "Give me some plow work, please. I have never yet given anything to my church that cost me anything."

In Bible days the most helpless, destitute, defenseless, dependable people were the widows. Elijah in 1 Kings 17 came to a widow that was down to less then necessities. Yet, this destitute person was called to relinquish the last bit of food that she had for her and her son. Miracle of miracles, upon giving out of this necessity she had an abundance for as long as needed. Later she was asked to give up her son. Denial upon denial! Do you think that this widow could have trusted God with her son if she had not been able to trust Him for her supper? Self-denial seemed to be the point where God broke in. Her result was joy, over both supper and son!

Further, we remember "the poor widow" in Mark 12:43 who in fact gave up her essentials. The poor widow did not have much but when she dug into self, God used this example to glorify Himself. This is exactly what is about to happen when God calls upon the servant/intercessor to deny himself for Christ and the gospel's sake.

> And he said unto them, When I sent you without purse, and scrip, and shoes, lacked ye any thing? And they said, Nothing (Luke 22:35).

23 | SACRIFICE

An ad read, "WANTED: wicks, to burn out for God. OIL AND LAMP SUPPLIED." This meant that we are to be willing to be the wick, and God will furnish the rest. John 5:35 speaks of "a burning and a shining light." All of us seem to want to shine, but few are willing to do what it takes—burn. The word *sacrifice* means being consumed in the hand of God!

If we are going to be a worthwhile and acceptable sacrifice we have to be willing to deny ourselves. The Old Testament lamb was given up by the family—denial. In the New Testament, God's Lamb was given up by the Father—denial. Sometimes it is difficult to distinguish between sacrifice and self-denial. To me self-denial is the walkway which leads to a worthy and acceptable sacrifice. Sacrifice speaks of the depths of self-denial. Sacrifice is the outside of an inside consecration.

We must not miss the clear difference between salvation and consecration. One is the appropriation of life while the other is the application of life. One is getting something and the other is giving something. One is what God does for us and the other is what God does through us (as in intercession). We are not sacrificing to become His but to, as one has explained, "deliver the goods" that have already been purchased. If one buys a valuable jewel at a store one expects to have it delivered upon call. Therefore self-denial and sacrifice are merely delivering goods into the hands of the Father upon His call, because they have already been purchased by Him!

If I as a servant/intercessor am to be willing and prepared to sacrifice I have some important questions that need to be answered.

> *Why* is the physical body so important in the sacrificial system?
> *What* kind of sacrifice is expected to be offered?
> *What* would cause any believer to want to be a sacrifice?
> *What* is required to get the body ready and prepared to sacrifice?
> *What* shall we do with our prepared sacrifice?
> *What* sort of situations demand a sacrifice?
> *What* is the result of being a living sacrifice?

Why is the body so important in the sacrificial system? (Rom. 12:1; Phil. 1:20; Heb. 10:5)—In Matthew 17:1-2, Christ's body is the place of the radiance and glory of God. His body became an outward reflection of an inward perfection of God's nature! Now you and I cannot show "perfection," but we can show the image of Christ and God's nature through our own bodies. The body is important because it contains that which is most valuable—the soul and spirit of the person. The soul and spirit are like the bejeweled intricate and intimate workings of a watch which requires a covering—the body.

When we read of God's "well-pleased" approval at Christ's transfiguration it reminds us that God said the same thing on the day of Jesus' bodily baptism. His body became a picture of the inward work of God. The body can and should reflect an already existing spiritual condition inside.

God is not dwelling in buildings. The body, according to 2 Corinthians 6:16, is a most important place because it is the temple of our spiritual life. The body is an instrument of human life and also of spirit life (Rom. 6:13). As an automobile is an instrument of the person at the controls—the inside/inner man—so is the physical body an instrument of the inner man.

The automobile goes where and how the person inside, the inner man, directs it. If the inner man directs the automobile on a crooked and dangerous course you can predict hurt and disaster. But if the inner man directs the automobile on a right and straight course you can predict just the opposite. God does not have our life unless He has our body! God does not have all (Luke 14:33) unless He has our body! There can be no happiness and little, if any, usefulness in half-hearted and half-surrendered Christianity.

If God does not have all of us we will be like the woman who testified to having barely enough religion to make her miserable. She had too much to be happy at the dance and too little to be happy at the prayer meeting. God is looking for all on the altar, not only part. The high priest in preparing for the ministry of sacrifice was anointed from head to foot—all. If we intend, as part of the priesthood of believers, to offer pleasing sacrifices (1 Pet. 2:5) to be consumed upon the altar and in the hands of God, it will require all of us, including the physical body.

In the Old Testament the sacrifice was dead animals but now Christ, living in us, calls for the basic sacrifice to be a living body reflecting His image through us as a Servant/Intercessor!

Come to think of it, our physical bodies are all we really have to sacrifice. The bondslave servant, on the auction block, when bought, did not stand before his master with great assets but often only his physical body. From that day on the servant would provide the body, and the master would furnish the provisions.

Oh, we like to think that we bring into the relationship with our Master great personality, ability, and the like. But the truth is, "Naked came I out of my mother's womb, and naked shall I return thither" (Job 1:21). While we are in this world, we are "all as an unclean thing, and all our righteousnesses are as filthy rags; and we all do fade as a leaf; and our iniquities, like the wind, have taken us away" (Isa. 64:6). When the Lord calls for our body to be sacrificed He is calling for the nearest, dearest thing that we have and the last thing we want to give up. It seems to me that if we are not willing to sacrifice the body, everything else, sooner or later, becomes contaminated. Our living is not at stake, but we are to live at the stake—daily upon a cross.

What are the kinds of sacrifice?—Even though we have spoken about giving one's life as a sacrifice, let us remember that this is the ultimate sacrifice that has been demonstrated by multiplied thousands of servants. To say that we are saved but have no willingness for our lives to be given up for Christ may mean that we have only met an evangelist, heard a sermon, or been to church, and never really met Christ. Richard Wurmbrand tells the story of a man who was so sad after he was saved. This prisoner had been told the story of Jesus who laid down His life that another's life might be saved. The prisoner had gladly received Christ but was now very sad. Upon being asked why he was sad, although he was saved, the prisoner responded by saying, "I can never be happy until I too have laid down my life for a friend." What this man was saying is that he had met Christ as Savior, full force, and he wanted to be like Jesus.

There is an old story about two brothers. There was a younger brother who was rebellious and wayward. He had no relationship with God or to an older brother who had accepted Christ and had become a godly man. The younger brother broke through the door of the older brother's home, his clothes stained with the blood of the man that he had just murdered. He explained to his older brother that he was being chased by the police and would surely go to prison and die if caught.

The older brother exchanged his clean clothes with the younger brother and put on the younger brother's blood-stained clothing. The younger brother hid in the back of the house wearing the clean clothes. The authorities came through the door and without any questions immediately apprehended and took away the man in the blood-stained clothes. The older brother in the blood-stained clothes, although innocent, was sentenced to die. At the moment of his execution he asked that a letter be passed to his younger brother at his death. The younger brother received the letter, which read, "Dear brother, even though I am innocent of your crime, I have taken your blood-stained clothes and given you my clean garments. I now gladly die in your place. But please, if you are ever tempted to turn back to the old life, remember that you are there because of my death and you are wearing my clean clothes."

The servant is to be willing to lay down his life in self-denial as a sacrifice because, in fact, he would have no life if it were not for Christ. Self-denial and sacrifice are brought together in the statement, "I will offer no sacrifice that costs me nothing" (see 2 Sam. 24:24; 1 Chron. 21:24).

What reason will daily motivate us to be willing to live a sacrificial life?—There is but one answer to that—the; mercies of God (Rom. 12:1; 2 Cor. 1:3; Rom. 9:15; Eph. 2:4; Jas. 5:11). How fitting! It was mercy that paid the price for us, and now it is the same mercy that draws us to the doorpost (Ex. 21:5). And that same mercy is calling us to daily sacrifice. The servant does not appeal upon the basis of the Master's power and authority but upon His immense mercy. If we came to Christ in mercy, are we willing now to go to the doorpost in mercy and daily stay upon the altar because of His mercies?

> I beseech you therefore, brethren, by the mercies of God, that ye present your bodies a living sacrifice, holy, acceptable unto God, which is your reasonable service (Rom. 12:1).

The priest of old used the "fleshhook" (Ex. 27:3; 1 Chron. 28:17; Num. 4:14) to keep the sacrifice in its place upon the altar. Praise God the hooks of our High Priest are not of cold, cruel metal but of His tender, kind mercies!

What are these holy hooks of tender, kind mercies? The word "therefore" in the beginning text refers to the explanation that lies in chapters 1—8 concerning the principles, teachings, dogma, belief, tenets, and doctrine of our faith. We will find these tender, kind mercies to be: deliverance from condemnation (Rom. 3:9-18), the gift of salvation (8:10-11), justification (3:24), sanctification (6:4), and glorification (8:28-39).

Millions have ruptured and ruined their lives and sold their souls for treasures of this world. But nothing can compare to the mercies of God that will allow us one day to step into glorified bodies in a glorified place and into His glorified presence. When I think of all of His tender, kind mercies I feel like shouting, "glory, glory, glory!" Dear friend, when we see the mercies of God we should be willing to place our bodies on the altar daily for Him. "I beseech you therefore, brethren, by the mercies of God, that ye present your bodies a living sacrifice, holy, acceptable unto God, which is your reasonable service" (Rom. 12:1).

This is the heavy question that cries for an answer! "How am I to prepare my body to daily be an acceptable, living sacrifice?" We must grasp what I would call the "process of preparation" that the body must follow as a living sacrifice upon the daily altar. Our text outlines three plain steps. First, we renew our minds. (Caution here, this is in no way referring to some intellectual approach to salvation and a changed life. This must be clearly understood.) After the renewing of the mind there is to be the transformed life. Then we are ready to present our bodies a living sacrifice. Thus, three steps are involved in the process of preparation:

1. Renewed mind
2. Transformed life
3. Presented bodies

Daily living the transformed life is the basic requirement of presenting our bodies daily as an acceptable living sacrifice. But we must not miss the first step because the renewing of the mind daily is what prepares us to live this all-important transformed life. Preparation for the daily sacrifice *begins* at renewing. We must not forget this! (Do you see how we have come back to the principle of "feeding" the new man as well as the three essential elements of intimacy?)

Someone would say, "Well, then let us get on to understanding about this renewing!" We should, but first we must deal with a most deadly difficulty. That difficulty is "daily." Yes, "daily" is the proverbial fly in the ointment. Since daily we live in this world and daily we are confronted with the altar of God and daily we brush up against the unacceptable trash of this life, it is then expected that we will daily need to enter into this process of preparation. Daily renewing will lead to daily transforming which will lead to daily presenting our bodies as a living sacrifice, holy and acceptable unto God. In self-defense the "old man" may squirm at the thought of "daily" and counter with a question, "What if I do not do this daily but only occasionally or sometimes? Aren't those occasional times acceptable unto God?" Frankly, I'm not certain exactly how God would view such half-hearted commitment. But I am absolutely certain about at least three facts along such a line of thinking.

1. I'm certain that God desires our sacrifice "daily."
2. I'm certain that all the days we don't enter into this process of preparation for daily sacrifice won't be accepted by God as living sacrifices. (If we don't, God won't!)
3. I'm certain it takes only one day, or even less, of unacceptable living in this world to ruin everything and everybody around you!

Let us determine "daily!" "Daily" is the call of God. May it then be the "daily" commitment of the servant/intercessor!

This process of preparation is easily observed in the life of Christ and others. Undoubtedly, Jesus was daily renewing Himself before the Father (Matt. 14:23). Although Christ did not need, as we, to continually be transformed daily because He was the incarnate God, nonetheless He was daily submitting to the will of the Father through His transformed life. And it is overwhelmingly obvious that Jesus was daily presenting His body a living sacrifice until it became a dead sacrifice. (Hallelujah, the altar of sacrifice was the doorway to the resurrected life!) Paul's life clearly demonstrates this process of preparation. He was daily renewing, "I die daily" (1 Cor. 15:31). He was endeavoring to live the transformed life, daily (Gal. 2:20). This process led him to be prepared to live daily as a sacrifice, and he wore the marks of proof (Gal. 6:14-17). Many, such as the martyrs, the suffering church, and a host of other dedicated believers have followed this process and thereby presented themselves as living sacrifices. How did they become martyrs, persecuted, ridiculed and discriminated against? Simply because they determined daily to live a transformed life and not be conformed to the world. This was because they were daily renewing in the Lord and consequently they were prepared as servant/intercessors to present their bodies as living sacrifices holy and acceptable unto God! Beloved, don't you know that when our Sovereign God reached down and enfolded Jesus, and later Paul and then others unto Himself, that all of heaven must have heard His voice whisper, "What an acceptable sacrifice!"?

Is God still looking for such believers today? Undoubtedly, and I believe that this process of preparation is essential for those who would be the *doulos*/intercessor.

What shall we do with our prepared sacrifice?

> I beseech you therefore, brethren, by the mercies of God, that ye present your bodies a living sacrifice, holy, acceptable unto God, which is your reasonable service (Rom. 12:1).

Already we have seen that the physical body is extremely important as a living sacrifice. The automobile is an instrument of the man inside it; the physical body is an instrument of spiritual life. (It may be one of wicked or godly design.) Nevertheless our physical body is the instrument and conveyance of our spiritual life. Further, we have come to be motivated to present our bodies as a living sacrifice by the "mercies of God."

We have discovered the beginning of sacrifice, the body of sacrifice, the reason of sacrifice, and the preparation for sacrifice. However, once the sacrifice has been prepared and is, in fact, transformed and fit for consumption in the hand and upon the altar of God, what shall we then do with our offering? We shall present it! Hallelujah, we shall present it!

"Present" means to put at one's disposal or to yield up. This is the same word which is translated "yield" in Romans 6:13,16,19. It is the technical term of presenting the Levitical victim and offering upon the altar of sacrifice. This is exactly the term of Luke 2:22 when Jesus' parents brought him to the temple to "present him to the Lord." What a thought, God bids us to come each day and do as was done with Christ before the Father! But such a desire of God should be no wonder to us because the transformed life is one where we have decreased and Christ has increased. What makes the transformed believer so appealing, acceptable, and holy to the hand and altar of God is that God sees Jesus! Consequently, we must know that when our flesh begins to preoccupy our bodies and God sees us thinking more of self than His dear Son, we in that moment become unfit sacrifices.

We are familiar with the practice of gifts being presented at Christmas, anniversaries, and birthdays—we call them presents. When we think of a sacrifice being presented in the Old Testament we, of course, think of the lamb being led to the altar or perhaps Abraham's only son Isaac willfully presenting himself as a sacrifice for the Father's will. In the New Testament I think of the wise men coming to the baby Jesus, desiring to present not only gifts but themselves to the Lord. And of course we cannot help but think of the ultimate presentation of a sacrifice, the Lamb of God. For we remember that *no one* took Jesus' life from Him. He said, "I lay it down of myself" (John 10:18).

There is always a question when we go to purchase a present to give. We find ourselves asking, "Will they like this, do you think they will like it?" Then when we give the gift we say, "I hope you like it. I hope this is what you wanted." There was also a big question in the heart of everyone in Old Testament days that made their way toward the altar of the temple with their sacrifice. It was the same question for one and all who took seriously their sacrifice and their relationship with God. Each kept asking themselves on the way to the altar, "Will my sacrifice be *acceptable* to God?" Frankly, I feel, for the most, this is a lost question in today's Christianity. Few of us are earnestly asking, "Is my life, as a daily, living sacrifice, really being acceptable unto God?" Much of this casual, thoughtless, careless, carefree, unmeasured, unexamined approach to God is the fault of many preachers and teachers and other Christians who have given the idea that God is just thrilled beyond words to receive any sort of help, regardless of the condition of the helper! Nothing could be further from the truth, as we will see from the Book of Malachi.

The reason those on the way to make their sacrifice kept asking the question, "Will this sacrifice be acceptable to God," was because they were well aware that some sacrifices were not acceptable to God. There are a number of texts that tell of God's renunciation of unacceptable sacrifices. Proverbs 15:8; Ecclesiastes 5:1; Jeremiah 6:20; Isaiah 1:11-15; and Matthew 5:23-24 are based upon an unacceptable offering. No passage in the Bible could more clearly reveal God's disdain for unacceptable sacrifices than Malachi 1:6-14. "A son honors his father, a servant honors his master. I am your Father and Master, yet you don't honor me. O priests, you despise my name" (v. 6, author).

"Who? Us?" you say, "When did we ever despise your name?"

"When you offer polluted sacrifices on My altar."

"Polluted sacrifices? When have we ever done a thing like that?"

"Every time you say, 'Don't bother bringing anything very valuable to offer to God.' You tell the people, 'Lame animals are all right to offer on the altar of the Lord—yes, even the sick and the blind ones.' And you claim this isn't evil? . . .

"'God, have mercy, on us,' you recite; 'God, be gracious to us!' But when you bring that kind of gift, why should He show you any favor at all?

" 'Oh, to find one priest among you who would shut the doors and refuse this kind of sacrifice. I have no pleasure in you,' says the Lord of hosts. 'And I will not accept your offerings.

"'But my name will be honored by the Gentiles from morning till night. All around the world they will offer sweet incense and pure offerings in honor of my name. For my name shall be great among the nations,' says the Lord of Hosts. 'But you dishonor it, saying that my altar is not important, and encouraging people to bring cheap, sick animals to offer to me on it.'

"You say, 'Oh, it's too difficult to serve the Lord and do what He asks.' And you turn up your noses at the rules He has given you to obey. Think of it! Stolen animals, lame and sick—as offerings to God! Should I accept such offerings as these?' asks the Lord. 'Cursed is that man who promises a fine ram from his flock, and substitutes a sick one to sacrifice to God. For I am a

Great King,' says the Lord of Hosts, 'and my name is to be mightily revered among the Gentiles'" (TLB).

Someone might claim that this is leaning too heavily upon the Old Testament sacrificial system. Please remember that the God of the Old Testament is the God of the New Testament and today. There is no doubt that the reference to sacrifice in Romans 12:1-2 is a direct link to the historical background of Old Testament sacrifice.

Not only can there be sacrifices offered by the believer that are not acceptable unto God, but also such unacceptable sacrifices can be extremely costly. Returning in *The Living Bible* to Malachi 2:1-4 makes this plain.

> Listen, you priests, to this warning from the Lord of Hosts: "If you don't change your ways and give glory to my name, then I will send terrible punishment upon you, and instead of giving you blessings as I would like to, I will turn on you with curses. Indeed, I have cursed you already because you haven't taken seriously the things that are most important to me. Take note that I will rebuke your children and I will spread on your faces the manure of these animals you offer me, and throw you out like dung. Then at last you will know it was I who sent you this warning to return to the laws I gave your father Levi," says the Lord of Hosts.

In the New Testament Book of Acts, God clearly demonstrates what he meant in Malachi 2:1-4 by taking the lives of both Ananias and Sapphira because of an unacceptable offering! Dear friends, we need to remember that it's still costly to try to offer unacceptable sacrifices to a living, holy God! We wonder why so many Christian homes are hurting and fragmented, why so many Christian children are rebellious and prodigal, why a so-called Christian nation like America is sinking and drowning in immorality and debauchery, why Christian individuals lead such roller-coaster lives and are often engaged in the most despicable sins. I am convinced that some of the reasons for all this is that we have been offering unacceptable sacrifices in our daily living and

God has rejected them and thrown them back into our faces! It matters not whether pastor, deacon, church, friends, or family accept our life as being Christian and godly. It is God that must be pleased and accept our sacrifice or all else is in vain!

While grilling outside, have you ever accidentally dropped a piece of meat onto the grass and then made an attempt to brush it off and place it again on the grill, hoping that it was clean enough to be acceptable to your guests? Later, you were horrified as someone excused themselves from the table, to spit out and reject the food because of the trash that remained on it, despite its deceiving appearance. The trash made it unacceptable. Beloved, the altar is not a place to burn off sin but a place to burn up a *prepared* sacrifice! Little wonder that David said he would take no offering to the Lord that did not cost him something (2 Sam. 24:24).

What is the result of being a living sacrifice? Worship! Yes, as we present our transformed lives to God for sacrifice this is an act of worship. We get the idea that worship is always sitting on padded pews with hands folded, gazing skyward through stained glass. That may be so, but that certainly is not the prerequisite or the fullness of worship. Worship is far more than mood music and catchy choruses. True worship is connected to daily living of the sacrificial life.

The life of Christ, the transformed life, is a life of *alternating*. Alternating between *solitude* with the Lord and *serving* and *interceding* actively among others in the world. Both of these acts are, in fact, worship. One cannot be substituted for the other any more than a monastery can be a substitute for a mission field or active duty a substitute for solitary confinement. We do not just walk *into* worship but we do walk *in* worship. God is manifested in our collective meetings in direct proportion to how He has been allowed to transform our lives daily. We need to forsake the notion that we can suddenly "work up" true worship or that we can simply run in and get a "quick fix" of worship. Real collective worship is experienced when pastor and people, living transformed lives of worship in solitude and service, come together in collective, transformed power. (I believe that, in part, this situation explains the deaths of Ananias and Sapphira. The church was living in such a transformed state after its beginning at Pentecost that such pretense was struck down by the holiness of God!) The lack of transformed lives in daily sacrifice on behalf of pastor, staff, and members also may explain why our assemblies are more conscious of time, detail, and facilities than the presence of God Himself. "Worship leader" is a buzz word today in church circles that refers to those on the platform during church services, when, in truth, the real worship leaders of any assembly of believers are those who come in from daily worshiping through transformed lives that have been consumed daily in the hand of God as a living sacrifice. Of course, this should be true of those on the platform although that may not always be the case. The power of God will be experienced and manifested in direct relationship with these transformed believers. Now, of course, it is possible to have a great crowd and a glorified "hootenanny" but that does not necessarily justify true worship.

The main point is that when transformed lives become sacrifices and are used daily by God, those acts become acts of worship. Worship is most often action. The sense of this action in worship is caught in 1 Peter 2:5. Here the priesthood of the believer's responsibility is spelled out. They are to offer spiritual sacrifices that are acceptable unto God through Christ. The priesthood of believers is not to reinterpret Scripture or to turn the believer loose to do anything one wants, but rather it is to use one's own body as a spiritual sacrifice on the daily altar. It is amazing how often we cry for the privilege of priesthood but how seldom we want to present our bodies sacrificially as a responsible priest.

This active presentation of our living bodies upon the daily altar, as an act of worship, may occur anywhere. It may be wiping the saliva and oatmeal from the chin of a stroke patient, giving a cup of cold water, soul-winning, studying, teaching, preaching, praying, and the like. What makes this a true act of worship is that it comes from a renewed, transformed life that is seen fit to be used by God as a servant interceding to glorify Himself. Colossians 3:17,23 gives us the difference between a mere kind, humanitarian act and a true act of worship before the God of the universe. So then, we should take all the tasks of every day; the ordinary work of the factory, job, school, market, whatever, and through a renewed, transformed life as a servant/intercessor, present it as an act of worship.

But now let us consider another most glorious truth. The sacrifice is to be a *voluntary* sacrifice. We are to consider the compassion and mercy of God upon us and then voluntarily present our bodies a living sacrifice. In the Old Testament, the sacrificial lamb had no choice and most likely was often dragged to the altar or deceived and misled. But no so with us!

If Christ has so increased in us as to make us a fit, transformed sacrifice then we will go willingly and voluntarily to the daily altar! We would expect such an agreeable action from within because this same Jesus that lives in us and is now so increased in us, has been down the street of sacrifice many times before.

In fact, if the struggle of trying to get to the altar of daily sacrifice is too fierce such is probably an indication that the flesh is trying to drag an unfit sacrifice to the altar—rather than God's lamb going voluntarily because of a transformed life. The Holy Spirit and Christ will press and plead but will never violate our will. Jesus' yearning voice underlines the importance of our volunteer action, "Oh, Jerusalem, Jerusalem, . . . how often would I have gathered thy children together, even as a hen gathereth her chickens under her wings, *and ye would not!*" (Matt. 23:37, author's italics).

24 | SUFFERING

For unto you it is given in the behalf of Christ, not only to believe on him, but also to suffer for his sake (Phil. 1:29).

We are reminded that in the servants' quarters we will invariably pass through three doors of self-denial, sacrifice, and suffering. Those who choose to dwell for any length of time in these quarters will find themselves, as a servant/intercessor, often passing over the threshold of the door called suffering, just as Jesus did.

Upon hearing of the splendor of a well-known Southern mansion compared with the cold meagerness of its servants' quarters, I mused aloud, "Surely the owner must never have come down from all of his splendrous living to visit the servants' quarters, otherwise the servants would have fared better because of an understanding master." It is a thrill to know that everyone who seeks to serve the Lord Jesus as their Master can have confidence in the fact that He, too, has come down and lived in these same quarters and passed through these same doors, especially the one entitled suffering (Heb. 2:11,14,16-18; 5:8). Yes, God has come down and entered man's skin to know his hunger, fear, hurt, thirst, agony, temptation, and even physical death. The missionary/camp song "Kum Ba Yah" (Come By Here) calls out to heaven in one of its verses, "Someone's crying, Lord." As we face suffering we know that the Lord has been by here and said, "Lo, I am with you alway" (Matt. 28:20).

Suffering Is Unavoidable

Suffering is the common ground and denominator for all people. It is no respecter of persons. Suffering is unavoidable. It will come! It may not come as soon, as deep, last as long, or be the same type that others experience (or it may come even sooner, deeper, longer) but it is sure to come. Someone has said, "the thorn room is just outside of the throne room." Therefore, the servant/intercessor realizes that the door marked suffering must be passed through. Some may read these lines to find a way to escape suffering in this human existence but that is not possible. Suffering will come! Our goal is to seize it, embrace it, and milk it dry of every eternal drop it is worth! And suffering does have great eternal worth! If Christ as Servant/Intercessor could not accomplish God's goal without suffering, can we? The unavoidable valley of suffering is as much a part of God's plan for the servant/intercessor as the mountaintop victories. "For unto you it is given in the behalf of Christ, not only to believe on him, but also to suffer for his sake" (Phil 1:29). "Wherefore let them that suffer according to the will of God commit the keeping of their souls to him in well-doing, as unto a faithful Creator (1 Pet. 4:19).

Two Forms of Suffering

Suffering is unavoidable to both the saved and the lost. Suffering comes generally in two forms to both the saved and the unsaved. There is the unpredictable suffering which is unforeseen. And there is the predictable suffering which is foreseen. Since the believer is our focus, let me illustrate these two in the believer who is committed to the servant/intercessor life.

Unpredictable suffering could come to the servant/intercessor in the form of cancer, AIDS, financial reversal, or loss of a loved one, all of which would be unforeseeable and thus unpredictable. (Perhaps Job's suffering fits best in this category.)

Predictable suffering is out there also. Believers may predict the same sort of suffering as was just listed if they persist in following Christ as a servant/intercessor. I know of a family, who upon the call of God, moved into a heavily contaminated industrial area where the majority of the population has contracted cancer and is dying. Thus, these servant/intercessors may predict the same sort of suffering. There is a missionary medical doctor that feels led of God to continue at his post doing blood work and surgery under the most primitive conditions among people of whom the majority are dying of AIDS. This servant/intercessor is likely facing predictable suffering. Legions of the faithful have lost jobs and promotions, predictably, because they were determined to stand for Christ. Many others have been able to foresee and predict the loss of loved ones in that their families, sweethearts, and friends, either turned their backs on them or they were left behind that they might take up the servant/intercessor's call of Christ. Undoubtedly, all can clearly see this predictable suffering in the lives of Paul, Stephen, Jesus, the martyrs, many Old Testament saints, and others of this present age.

What shall we do? If unpredictable suffering befalls us, we will use it. If predictable suffering is seen, we will not draw back from it, because the servant/intercessor, who understands and accepts the work and ministry of suffering, knows there are hidden treasures to be found in suffering, both unpredictable as well as predictable.

Suffering's Effect upon the Unseen World

Before we go further, let us consider a great spiritual truth that is seldom understood in the course of the believer's suffering. How does the believer's suffering on earth affect the unseen spiritual world? Dr. Josef Tson of the Romanian Missionary Society in Wheaton, Illinois, uses the account of Job to clarify this point. Dr. Tson released a tremendous book on *The Theology of Martyrdom*.[14]

The story of Job opens a door for us to see what is going on in the spiritual world. There was a meeting. Satan was there with his people, his angels, and God announced to everybody that

Job was a totally righteous person—absolutely righteous. Satan could not challenge the statement of God. Job was indeed righteous. But you know Satan always finds fault and accuses falsely what is right. So he made a false accusation against Job. "What is Job's motivation for worshiping You, God, and for being righteous? His motivation is the riches You give him. Of course, he can afford to be righteous when You make him the richest man in the land. Who wouldn't worship You for that?"

Satan says, "In order to see that I am right, take away all that You gave him and he will curse you. That will prove that his worship to You is worthless, because You only bribe him into worshiping you. God, You buy his worship with goods and things." Such was the meaning and content of Satan's false accusation.

Suddenly, all of heaven was frozen in horror. God's honor was at stake. There was only one way to defend God's honor. There was only one person in the whole world who could uplift God's honor—Job. God had no other way but to say to Satan, "Go down and take away absolutely all I gave Job and let's see his reaction." And just imagine now all of heaven was watching to see the reaction. There were those messengers coming to Job. There were tornadoes after tornadoes that destroyed all that Job had. The messengers were coming one after another to tell him that his cattle, camels, and donkeys were gone. Eventually his houses were gone, and his ten children were dead.

At that moment all heaven was watching the lips of Job—the man who was standing tall under all that horror, suffering, and grief. Then Job's quivering lips began to murmur: "God has given; God has taken away; God's name be . . . (and all of heaven was waiting, because Satan had said that God would be cursed) . . . God's name be praised!" At that moment all of heaven began to shout!

But Satan said, "Stop, it's not over. You see, he is still healthy. He can still enjoy life, and if he is a selfish person he will be able to forget about all of his losses and with his health he can still be happy. But let me touch his skin and cause him to suffer. Let his body be caught in excruciating pain and he will become the most miserable person in all the land, and he will curse You then." Again, God's honor was at stake. Again, all of heaven was watching. And that day God said, "Go ahead and bring suffering." Job was suddenly covered with boils. And everybody was so afraid of him I can imagine they took him out of the city and threw him out on the garbage heap, and there he scratched his wounds and the dogs came and licked his sores. He was the most miserable man in all the world. Then his wife came and said, "Don't you see, there is only one way out of this. Curse God, and die" (see 2:9). The poor woman did not realize that she was encouraging her husband to do exactly what Satan desired. Then his so-called friends came to comfort him but instead they accused him. Again and again, they brought up the issue, "Now, how are you with God?"

Finally Job said, "Let me clarify this matter for everyone who watches. I don't know why God has allowed this suffering to come to me and I don't understand it. I wish I knew the answers. But let me tell you my attitude toward God during this suffering, Even if it appears that God kills me, I still intend to trust Him and praise Him!" At that moment it was all over in heaven! It was all settled. The entire spiritual world, both godly and satanic, had seen clearly by a righteous man's suffering that God was right and Satan was wrong. God got the victory, and Satan was put to shame in front of all heaven which was shouting the victory. Satan had to run from that in defeat.

A most important point to remember is that Job never really knew how tremendously important it was that his response during his suffering be one of faithfulness, praise, and trust to God, thereby defeating Satan with shame and causing heaven to shout. He could not dream or even imagine that his response to suffering would have such an extraordinarily glorious effect upon the unseen spiritual world!

The evidences of Scripture lead us to the conviction that every time a believer suffers today the unseen spiritual world watches and waits to see our response. Tson went on to note that we are a part of the display for victory in the arena of spiritual warfare as we suffer. First Corinthians 4:9 says that the believer is "a spectacle." The word for "spectacle" is the word from which we get the word *theater* [*theatron*]. The believer, in his suffering, is upon a cosmic amphitheater before both the unseen angels and seen men (Eph. 6:12; 3:10). Then what shall we do but look to Jesus as our example and pattern for victorious suffering? First Peter 4:1 and 2:21 are explicit. The word "example" in 1 Peter 2:21 is the word used to describe the line that the teacher writes at the top of the slate for the student to imitate in their own writing. Jesus wrote the first perfect and beautiful line of how we are to respond in suffering. Now as servants committed to His likeness, we are to imitate that pattern, that example. "He that saith he abideth in him ought himself also so to walk, even as he walked" (1 John 2:6). Christ's suffering should strengthen the body and stimulate the church.

"Let your light so shine before men, that they may see your good works, and glorify your Father" (Matt. 5:16). Most of us are willing to shine and show in our attendance, singing, preaching, teaching, giving, witnessing, and so forth, and that is as it should be. However, are we willing to shine and show in suffering as we follow the path of Christ? Most of us are willing to conform to the likeness of Christ in love, joy, peace, and that is as it should be. But are we not also obligated to conform to the likeness of Christ in suffering? The answer is yes, because suffering is the most arresting scene in the *theatron*, "spectacle" of our lives. It always draws intense attention from the seen and the unseen.

It seems to me we have come to an era where all the sects, religions, and even cults are using the same jargon. The lost world is confused by the same music coming out of so many obviously different horns. One theologian wrote, "There are times in which lectures and publications no longer suffice to communicate the necessary truth. At such times, the deeds and sufferings of the saints must create a new alphabet in order to reveal again the secret of truth." And, no doubt, obedience is the essence of this persuasive language!

Why Does God Not Protect His Followers from Suffering?

The truth is that God does protect us from much suffering, but not all. God allows unavoidable suffering to come to even His most righteous followers because He is more concerned about our spiritual well-being than He is about our physical health. And suffering is a useful aid to spiritual health.

The Purpose of Suffering

To me there are at least three obvious biblical purposes for God to allow suffering to come to the believer's life.

1. To *shape* the believer.
2. To *strengthen* the body.
3. To *save* the lost.

Of course, these three things may be accomplished in other ways without suffering. However, nothing is quite as forceful as suffering to produce these three spiritual results.

Jesus is the magnificent example of these three purposes being accomplished through the Suffering Servant. Christ was *shaped* and formed perfectly to the Father's will. His suffering not only *strengthened* the brethren but it started the body—the church. It was the atoning death, with its suffering, that saved the lost. We now are to allow Jesus, who dwells in our own flesh and blood, to use our suffering much as He did in His own flesh and blood. Of course, there is only one atonement, but the believer's suffering can be used by Christ to bring the lost to salvation.

Think of that! Omnipotent God has taken unavoidable suffering that was originally meant for evil and has now turned it to glorious and eternal good! Think of that!

Suffering Shapes the Believer

And we know that all things work together for good to them that love God, to them who are the called according to his purpose. For whom he did foreknow, he also did predestinate to be conformed to the image of his son, that he might be the firstborn among many brethren (Rom. 8:28-29).

"I am the true vine, and my Father is the husbandman" (John 15:1) brings us to the sharpest focus upon the life of the believer. The shaping of the believer's life to be like Christ begins and ends with the cutting of the branches. You mean we must go looking for suffering? No, suffering is already looking for us. And when suffering finds us, in that moment, hour, day, or year, which we often have dreaded and attempted to dodge, we will find that suffering will bring the possibility of great gifts to shape us into the likeness of Christ!

God is looking for "fruit." He is not looking for suckers, runners, shade, leaves, or even beauty—but fruit. "Fruit" is the Master's mark, the believer's badge, the Almighty's authentication. But what does fruit authenticate? I see three things:

1. *"Some" fruit* indicates to me that a person is saved. All saved people will produce some fruit even though it may be tiny, shriveled, and sour.
2. *"More" fruit* authenticates a deeper commitment. "And every branch that beareth fruit, he purgeth it, that it may bring forth more fruit" (v. 2b). The more committed believer will produce more fruit than just some fruit.
3. *"Much" fruit* indicates a believer that is being mastered and matured as a "father" in the faith. "Herein is my Father glorified, that ye bear much fruit; so shall ye be my disciples" (v. 8). And this fruit is described in Galatians 5:22; Hebrews 12:11; Ephesians 5:9; and Philippians 1:9-11. Isn't it clear that the servant/intercessor must have such fruit? God intends to aid us in bearing such needful fruit by using the one thing that is unavoidable—suffering, the very thing that we dread and dodge. He will use this not to hurt, but to help us here and now and for all eternity!

The profound secret of this glorious fruitbearing is: it is not to be grafted on from the outside, but to be let out from the inside.

Remember, this is the fruit of the "Suffering Servant," this is His sap in us, the branches! When we are cut, bruised, skinned, battered, suffering, those times afford us our greatest opportunity for the essence—the sap—of the Suffering Servant to come forward. When the world stabbed the Suffering Servant blood and water came forth. When the world stabs us the Suffering Servant comes forth!

Fruit comes by pruning (John 15:2). Make no mistake about it. What someone has said is true, "Branches that bear fruit must get the knife." Some believer might say, "But I want to have the fruit without the suffering." That is understandable. I do believe it is possible for "some" fruit to come without suffering. We will find that it takes the scalpel to produce "more" and "much more" fruit. Diamonds do not dazzle with beauty unless they are cut. When cut, the rays of the sun fall on them and make them shine with wonderful colors. When we are cut by suffering we also should shine as jewels of the King as well as be shaped as a believer. Your brightest glow may come at the time and place when you are cut and suffer the deepest. I heard Leonard Ravenhill say that when his body had been terribly broken in an accident and he had spent many weeks of agonizing pain and suffering, an old missionary who had endured many years of torture, persecution, and suffering for Jesus came to his beside. The missionary, stooped and drawn because of his own suffering, only raised his hand over the body of Ravenhill and said, "All He is seeking is thy dross to come soon and thy gold to refine."

So it is true, suffering is really a refining and shaping instrument upon our spiritual life. Even as the suffering of the pruning knife produces the fruit, we become more like Him.

All will agree that suffering is a great equalizer. It is a common ground and a common denominator of all humankind. Yes, suffering is no respecter of persons; it comes to all. When suffering grips a Christian, he must come down out of his church tower. He can draw only so much from his little, happy, wholesome support group. He must come into the dark pit of suffering on his own, whether he is rich or poor, simple or sophisticated, lost or saved. The ground is level at the foot of the cross. Many would agree that it is also level in the emergency room. In that time of suffering the world stands by and says, "Let us see what Mr. Christian does now!"

The Purpose of Fruit

God's purpose is not to beautify man with fruit. His purpose is to use the fruit to conform man to the likeness of Christ. We know that Christ was and is the pure fruit. What happened to Him? God allowed His pure fruit to be squeezed by suffering! And when this true, pure fruit was squeezed out flowed "rivers of living waters" (John 7:38). This is exactly what was happening with Job. Satan was saying in effect, "Let him be squeezed by suffering and we will see what is really on the inside."

I have read that in communities where apples are grown, occasionally a tree gives all its energy to producing wood and leaves and bears no fruit. When that occurs, the orchardist makes a deep gash with an ax across the trunk of the tree and close to the ground. The result is the gash gives such a shock to the selfish tendencies of the tree that a positive change is brought about and the next year the tree bears much fine fruit. Now, do we see how essential suffering is to our shaping? It is the suffering of the pruning knife that produces the "more" and "much more" fruit of the likeness of Christ. It is suffering that so often squeezes the fruit that reveals the depth and richness of Christ in and through us. We must never forget that while suffering is shaping us as believers, we must keep our spiritual eyes focused on the future because we are also being prepared for all eternity (2 Cor. 4:16-18). In my understanding of the Scriptures, suffering not only produces fruit but it also proves the believer fit for coreigning and coruling in eternity as we observed in the quarry illustration found in chapter 14 under the Servant's View—The Earth (1 Pet. 2:5 and 1 Kings 6:7).

Suffering Strengthening the Body

But the God of all grace, who hath called us unto his eternal glory by Christ Jesus, after that ye have suffered a while, make you prefect, stablish, strengthen, settle you (1 Pet. 5:10).

Are suffering and pain important to a healthy body? Absolutely yes! Dr. Paul Brand in his book, *In His Image*, illustrates that the main problem of those suffering from leprosy is the very absence of pain and suffering. Suffering is, in fact, healthy for the body as you will see from this excerpt from Brand's book.

When Sadan first came to Vellore, his feet had shrunk to half their normal length and his fingers were shortened and paralyzed. It took us nearly two years of unflagging effort to stop the pattern of destruction in his feet. Meanwhile we began reconstructing his hands, a finger at a time, attaching the most useful tendons to the most useful digits and retraining his mind to control the new set of connections. In all, Sadan spent four years with me in rehabilitation. He personified the soft-spoken gentle Indian spirit. Together, we wept at our failures and rejoiced at the gradual successes. I came to love Sadan as a dear friend.

At last Sadan decided he should return home to his family in Madras for a trial weekend. He had come to us with badly ulcerated hands and feet. Now his hands were more flexible, and with a specially designed rocker-type shoe he could walk without damage. "I want to go back to where I was rejected before," he said proudly, referring to the cafes that had turned him away, and the buses that had denied him service. "Now that I am not so deformed I want to try my way in the great city of Madras."

Before Sadan left, we reviewed together all the dangers he might encounter. Since he had no warning system of pain, any sharp or hot object could harm him. Having learned to care for himself in our hospital and workshop, he felt confident. He boarded a train to Madras.

On Saturday night, after an exuberant reunion dinner with his family, Sadan went to his old room where he had not slept for four years. He lay down on the woven pallet on the floor and drifted off to sleep in great peace and contentment. At last he was home, fully accepted once again.

The next morning when Sadan awoke and examined himself, as he had been trained to do at the hospital, he recoiled in horror. Part of the back of his left index finger was mangled. He knew the culprit because he had seen many such injuries on other patients. Evidence was clear: telltale drops of blood, marks in the dust, and, of course, the decimated clump of tendon and flesh that had been so carefully reconstructed some months before. A rat had visited him during the night and gnawed his finger.

Immediately he thought, "What will Dr. Brand say?" All that day he agonized. He considered coming back to Vellore early, but finally decided he must keep his promise to stay the weekend. He looked in vain for a rat trap to protect him that last night at home but the shops were closed for a festival. He concluded he must stay awake to guard against further injury.

All Sunday night Sadan sat cross-legged on his pallet, his back against the wall, studying an accounting book by the light of a kerosene lantern. About four o'clock in the morning the subject drew dull and his eyes felt heavy and he could no longer fight off sleep. The book fell forward onto his knees and his hand slid over to one side against the hot glass of the hurricane lamp.

When Sadan awoke the next morning he saw instantly that a large patch of skin had burned off the back of his right hand. He sat trembling in bed, despair growing like a tumor inside him, as he stared at his two hands—one gnawed by a rat, the other melted down to the tendons. He had learned the dangers and difficulties of leprosy, in fact had taught them to others. Now, he was devastated by the sight of his two damaged hands.[15]

Brand's account dramatically emphasizes an important truth of the physical body that is also true to the spiritual body. Suffering is helpful to the body. It is clear in 1 Peter 5:10 that the Christian becomes more complete, more established, better founded, and strengthened *after* suffering. We are not only on display before the unseen world but we are also a "spectacle," *theatron*, before our fellow believers, the body. Ephesians 6:12 and 3:10 point out both "angels" and "men" look on.

Paul the apostle lived out his life and suffered many pains not only to be shaped as a believer but also that the body, the church, be strengthened. This tremendous truth is borne out in the accounts of Paul's life as reflected in 2 Corinthians 11:16-28; Philippians 1:11-18; Colossians 1:24. In addition to Paul, suffering that strengthens the believer can be seen in the life of Job, Jesus, the apostles, a multiplicity of biblical characters, and tens of thousands of others since Bible days. Such strengthening of the body, through suffering, still goes on this very moment. Many believers tell how they have been strengthened by the testimony of Joni Eareckson Tada, Corrie ten Boom, Josef Tson, Haralan Popov, and Richard Wurmbrand. Does not such deep spiritual victory in the face of agonizing suffering strengthen you? Of course it does. It will strengthen any part of the body that comes in contact with such!

Recently, I stood over the bed of a boyhood friend who for twenty-five years has suffered as a quadriplegic because of a tragic car accident. Don Smith's bed remains totally motionless— nothing moves at all, except his head. His lips move, I lean forward, and I hear these words, "Bobby, the joy of all of this suffering is that I have now found Christ as my Savior and I am truly happy. The happiest I have ever been!" Can you take that in! Now it is far clearer to me why his hospital room walls are completely covered with awards, decorations, and pictures of a successful football coach and a radiant Christian—all accomplished amid suffering. Does that not inspire and strengthen you? Of course it does. Such will strengthen any part of the body with which it comes in contact.

In this same Dublin, Georgia, Veterans Administration hospital, I move from Don's room, 19-A, down the hall to room 17-A where I meet Tommy Walker—a man cut down by a stroke in the prime of family life. Now hardly able to control any part of his body, confined to bed and chair, even without the ability to speak, Tommy communicates by holding a leather pad in his mouth. From this extends an eighteen-inch stick that is used to slowly eke out, from his healthy brain, his thoughts upon a small electronic display. I asked Tommy, "What good has come of this suffering?" He responded, "I would not have been saved if I had not had this suffering and now this suffering is being used 'to good that the gospel might be shared abroad'" (Rom. 5:1-5). It is little wonder that this brother compiles, types, and has printed, himself, a newsletter that goes out to several foreign countries and almost all the states. This newsletter of encouragement is appropriately entitled *SUNSHINE — For the glory of God and the teaching of the church.* Does that not strengthen you, dear believer? Of course it does and it will strengthen any other part of the body that comes in contact with such!

I have stood at the water's edge and read the wife's account where in 1958 a young missionary drowned in Africa. Seven years later a man went there to write the missionary's biography. As he prepared to write, another missionary came to him to show him the place where the young man drowned. "My wife and I are missionaries here because of this drowned man." Then someone else came and said, "I am here also because of this man's death, because in our seminary when the news broke that he had died there was an appeal made that someone enter the service in his place, and dozens of us accepted. We are everywhere in the world today because of this man's death." One man has been allowed to suffer death, and now many have been called out because of that suffering, to be a strength to the body.

I myself am in large part in the gospel ministry today, as well as many others who were called out, because of a pair of shoes that belonged to missionary Betty Smith. Her shoes were laid on an altar with an appeal for someone to go and take the place of this one who had died suddenly due to hardship in His service.

Aren't we all strengthened as a part of the body when we know of victorious suffering by believers? Such suffering for the strengthening of the body is a far cry from the usual whimpering and whining that so often goes on among believers at the least discomfort. May God have mercy on us for such misunderstandings of suffering and lead us to discover the hidden treasures of our suffering that we, the believer, may be shaped and that the body may be strengthened.

"As my Father hath sent me, even so send I you" (John 20:21), were Jesus' words to the disciples. So it is that you and I are sent to strengthen the church as we are observed even in our suffering. We suffer! We are squeezed! We are watched! And, by the grace of God, we remember all those that have gone before us, most especially Jesus; then we rise up victorious in our suffering! In our suffering we are shaped as believers, strengthened in the body, and are used to the saving of the lost. Heaven shouts because of the victory! And Something, Someone, inside of us shouts, Hallelujah! Hallelujah!

Suffering Saves the Lost

For as the sufferings of Christ abound in us, so our consolation also aboundeth by Christ. And whether we be afflicted, it is for your consolation and salvation, which is effectual in the enduring of the same sufferings which we also suffer: or whether we be comforted, it is for your consolation and salvation (2 Cor. 1:5-6).

But I would ye should understand, brethren, that the things which happened unto me have fallen out rather unto the furtherance of the gospel (Phil. 1:12).

Salvation by suffering is preached (Acts 17:3,6) and salvation by suffering is practiced (2 Cor. 1:5-10). We must be willing to use our suffering that the lost might be saved. Salvation comes by the suffering of Jesus (Heb. 2:9-14).

Do not misunderstand. It is *only* Christ's atoning death that secures the lost's salvation (Heb. 7:22-25; Isa. 53:10-11; Heb. 5:7-9). However, the suffering of a believer can be used greatly by God to draw the lost to the Savior's salvation. We know that in a healthy body of believers the whole body feels the suffering of the members. Therefore, the overwhelming tendency of the body of Christ is to help and strengthen itself. But the church must always intimately live close enough to the heart of Christ to also suffer for those outside the body. If we should ever wonder which is to have the priority of our sensitivity, all we need do is recall that there was no body or any members until first Christ suffered and died for the lost! Many seem to have forgotten this. The body of Christ is strengthened for *one reason*, to be healthy enough to suffer to the extent that the lost might be saved. This truth is the example of Jesus.

Why "equip the saints" to be servants/intercessors? To help lost man at his worst affliction—that of spiritual death. Too long, too many "super saints" have been rotting in their equipment, inside the church. The gifts, attitudes, fruits are all to be used ultimately to win the lost.

I, personally, am interested in my own physical health only to the extent that it makes me more able to spend myself for the cause of Christ—winning the lost. To give my health for the lost is not something I am to avoid but rather it is the reason I take care of my body. It is my conviction (based upon Matt. 19:29; 6:33; and Phil. 2:25-30) that if I seek health in order to help the kingdom then I may expect the Lord to work that to good for the sake of my wife, family, and quality of spiritual living while here on earth. In short, the surest way to salvage the best of this life for self and family is to try daily to spend your life for Christ.

How Does a Believer's Suffering Lead to the Saving of the Lost?

Therefore I endure all things for the elect's sakes, that they may also obtain the salvation which is in Christ Jesus with eternal glory (2 Tim. 2:10).

The purpose of God in human history is the salvation of the lost world. "God was in Christ, reconciling the world" (2 Cor. 5:19). Through Christ's suffering salvation is offered to the lost. Christ's suffering was a miraculous act of God *never to be repeated*.

But has God's purpose been accomplished yet? Is the world saved? Why not? The lost of the world remain unsaved because they have not yet obtained Christ's offered salvation. The believer's suffering is a way that Christ's salvation may be seen, grasped—obtained. This may be repeated again and again as the believer's sufferings become "colabored" (see 1 Cor. 3:9) with Christ and build upon His suffering. To be sure, the lost can be saved without the witness of a believer's suffering but there is no stronger or more convincing witness than the believer's suffering in the hands of God. Both 2 Timothy 2:10 and 2 Corinthians 1:6 are made clear in the light of this.

Paul suffered for the lost to be saved. He was the Antioch pastor. This was a rich town during some of the greatest times. The church had several pastors and organizations and things were growing and glowing. It was a great and glorious place to be serving. There came a day when Paul had to choose. Go or stay? Go meant suffering (2 Cor. 11:23). Paul went and God used the suffering that the lost might obtain the salvation offered in Jesus. Day by day Paul lived, preached, suffered, and the lost were drawn and saved! By his bonds and suffering the church was strengthened with boldness—resulting in the spreading of the gospel.

> But I would ye should understand, brethren, that the things which happened unto me have fallen out rather unto the furtherance of the gospel; So that my bonds in Christ are manifest in all the palace, and in all other places; And many of the brethren in the Lord, waxing confident by my bonds, are much more bold to speak the word without fear. Some indeed preach Christ even of envy and strife; and some also of good will: The one preach Christ of contention, not sincerely, supposing to add affliction to my bonds: But the other of love, knowing that I am set for the defense of the gospel. What then? notwithstanding, every way whether in pretense, or in truth, Christ is preached; and I therein do rejoice, yea, and will rejoice (Phil. 1:12-18).

First-century Christians suffering was the agent whereby the lost obtained salvation. During Nero's persecution (beginning in A.D. 60) a pattern was being established for the body of Christ. Once you became a believer you were most likely destined for suffering and death publicly, often in the jaws of the coliseum's lions. In dealing with their lot in life, these early believers grasped the truth of which we now study. Upon seeing their suffering and death as a divine privilege, they entered into it with singing and praise. Such an approach to suffering and death shocked the pagan world that inflicted the pain. Not only were the lost shocked, they began to search for the truth behind such an existence in the face of suffering and death. Results from such a search were many being saved.

The account of a pagan lawyer named Tertullian is just such a story. As Tertullian searched for what caused these believers to be so victorious in suffering, he discovered Christ and was converted. Later, he wrote a book on this subject and coined this expression, "The blood of Christians is seed."

Josef Tson refers to Augustine's view that the martyrs were bound, jailed, scourged, racked, burned, rent, butchered, and they multiplied. This is what I also heard recently from Harold Peasley of South Africa who quoted from a Communist document that read, "Be careful what you do with those called Christians because when they are made to suffer they then multiply."

There are so many illustrations of this miracle work. The suffering may come in many forms, especially including emotional suffering. Once a man told me of the most unbelievable and ungodly behavior of his wife. He concluded that he must endure this unspeakable suffering of the heart and emotions for one reason. The husband reasoned that God had called him to wrestle for his wife's soul. Such an unspeakable struggle of suffering reminded me of Jacob! The conclusion was that the woman was saved, their life and marriage became a heaven because through a believer's suffering one was delivered from hell.

Yes, the glorious truth is that the believer's suffering can be used by God to win the lost. What are you allowing God to do with your suffering?

A. Is suffering shaping you more like Jesus?
B. Are fellow Christians being strengthened because of your victory within this suffering?
C. Has anyone been saved as a result of your suffering?

EPILOGUE

ONE SEED ON OUR SAMARITAN ROAD
(ACTS 1:8)

Revival in our heart, home, and especially the Western world waits upon the followers of Christ to turn back to the life-style of Jesus. The opposite has been exhausted by the fake "prosperity gospel" along with a multitude of other shortcut attempts to spirituality and power with God.

The burned, parched, wounded lips of our world have never been more ready for plain, pure, uncontaminated living water. They will quickly recognize the real life of Christ in comparison to the mere mirages that have confused and led so many astray in a wilderness of false hope. The Sacrificed Servant/Intercessor life of Christ, through the believer, is the only way to a great awakening . . . and the time is ripe!

Our need is clearly expressed in the song that exclaims, "for the showers we plead." However, as an individual follower we must be willing to take our place as one solitary "mercy drop" that is falling. The question is, "Am I willing to be one sacrificed life for His glory here and hereafter?"

Many know of the tragic murder of missionary Lynda Bethea of Kenya at the hands of robbers who pretended to be injured travelers along an isolated mountain road. My son and I had made special efforts to go to the exact spot of her death shortly after. I stood at that spot in deep prayer of thanksgiving for her life and an inspiration of what really had actually occurred there.

205

In the early hours of the next morning I arose and wrote the following in my personal notes.

As I literally absorb the most unspeakable vista of the Rift Valley, which in part attracted Karen Blixen to this Eden of Africa, and glimpses of which made the movie *Out Of Africa* a classic of this continent. The differences seem almost too jarring to reconcile.

Not many nights before this picturesque, narrow, winding road was transformed from a "photo opportunity spot" into a "professor's opportunity spot." Yes, one who so beautifully professed Christ through her life and lips is suddenly confronted with the opportunity of "witness" in its fullest and deepest meaning of Acts 1:8.

An intrinsic impulse, born in the spirit of Christ and brought from the shoulder of the original Samaritan road, causes the traveler to stop to help, in the name of Christ, another on this road. However, upon this Kenyan road all roles are reversed—the one pretending injury is the robber and now the good Samaritan is to become the victim—of ambush and murder.

As Lynda leaped from that edge of Eden into the arms of Jesus she left on the shoulder of her Samaritan path that sacred seed which allows her into the most elite fellowship known—that of fellowshipping with Jesus in His suffering—even unto death.

Yes, how jarringly strange to us it is, that our Lord allows ordinary and cruel roads to wind so near to such unspeakable vistas of comfort and beauty where blessed blooms are collected and such sacred seed are sown.

We must never be intimidated by demons of darkness, no matter how subtle or sudden, to only walk on "the other side"—for we are but lambs of His pastures and seed for the sowing. And the gates of hell will not prevail against such, for all of heaven waits to shout . . . "Well done, good and faithful servant (doulos); thou hast been faithful over a few things, I will make thee ruler over many things: enter thou into the joy of thy Lord."

"As the Father sent me,

So I send you" (GNB).

NOTES

Chapter 16: Dangers

1. Norman Grubb, *Rees Howell, Intercessor* (London: Lutterworth Press, Cox and Wyman, Ltd., 1973), 101.
2. Ibid., 100.

Chapter 17: A Language

3. *Florida Baptist Witness*, Dec. 3, 1987, 4.
4. E. G. Carré, *Praying Hyde* (South Plainfield, NJ: Bridge Publishing, n.d.), 39.

Chapter 18: Brokenness

5. T. A. Hegne, *The Cross and Sanctification* (Minneapolis: Bethany House, 1960), 189.
6. Amy Carmichael, *Gold Cord* (Washington, PA: Christian Literature Crusade, 1932).

Chapter 19: Humility

7. Gayle Erwin, *Jesus Style* (Waco, TX: Word Books, 1983), 100.

Chapter 22: Self-denial

8. *Our Daily Bread* (booklet) (Grand Rapids, MI: Radio Bible Class, 1980), n.p.n.
9. J. Hudson Taylor, *Hudson Taylor* (Minneapolis: Bethany House, n.d.), 21.
10. Amy Carmichael, *Gold Cord* (Washington, PA: Christian Literature Crusade, 1932), 336.
11. *The Voice of the Martyrs* (Middlebury, IN: n.p., n.d.), 3.
12. Ronald J. Sider, *Rich Christians in the Age of Hunger* (London: Hodder and Stoughton, 1971), 17.
13. Ibid., 21.

Chapter 24: Suffering

14. Josef Tson, *A Theology of Martyrdom* (Wheaton, IL: Romanian Missionary Society, 1987), n.p.n.
15. Paul Brand and Philip Yancey, *In His Name* (Grand Rapids, MI: Zondervan, 1984), 239.